Newport's Story Retold
Mairi Shiels

Forgan Publishing

© Mairi Shiels 2016
Published by Forgan Publishing

ISBN: 978-1-5262-0513-1

Printed in Palatino 10pt

Text layout by Robertson Printers, Forfar
Cover design by Mairi Shiels and Robertson Printers, Forfar
Printed and bound in Great Britain by Robertson Printers, Forfar

ACKNOWLEDGEMENTS

Researching the material for this book has given me the greatest pleasure and enjoyment. This truly has been a labour of love! There are however certain people without whose help and assistance it might never have been completed. I sincerely hope I have missed no-one.

My grateful thanks therefore to the following, in no particular order other than alphabetical, who in some cases have taken considerable time and effort to advise and correct me: Betty Baxter; William Berry; Henry Burnett; Ron Caird; David Cowley; John Don; John Dott; Gordon Douglas; Betty Evans; Iain Gray; Mike Latto; Angie Livingstone; Linda McGill (Caston); Margaret McNicol; Andrew and Hilary Mylius; Adam Olejnik; Philip Owen; William Owen; Jeanette Storrier; Hamish Tough; Colin Vincent; Margaret and Bill Wright.

I must also thank my lovely mother, Elspeth McGregor, who at the age of 96 willingly volunteered to take on the onerous task of proof-reading the finished manuscript! Her grammar and spelling, so rigorously taught and diligently learned in Innerleithen School almost a century ago, still stand her in good stead today. We inevitably had some differences of opinion, but her enormous contribution is hugely appreciated.

Photo acknowledgements
For permission to reproduce photographs and pictures, thanks are extended to the following: William Berry (P21, P85, P87, P92, P93); Jean Campbell (P162); Nigel Clark (P178); Elizabeth Cuthbert (P147); Marianne Dee (P158); John Don (P19, P146); Dundee Libraries (P3, P28, P71,P100, P102, P145, P151); Fife Cultural Trust (P101); Gerd Garnes (P70, P78, P133, P137, P138); Stanley Gordon (P55); Sheena Gray (P135); Gordon Hogg (P179); J Johnstone (P148); Angie Livingstone (P154); David and Morag McLaren (P125, P142); Phil O'Hare (P38, P39, P43); Norma Roberts (P75); St Mary's Episcopal Church (P57); Fiona Scott-Barrett (P106); David Smith (P64, P121, P123); Silvie Taylor (P167): Tay Road Bridge Joint Board (P119, P120, P122, P126, P127); Margaret Wright (P114, P176).

Special thanks to Ian Lindsay who has been so generous in allowing me to freely browse and choose images from his wonderful postcard collection. Every effort has been made to ascertain ownership of photographs. Sincere apologies if any have not been appropriately acknowledged.

FOREWORD

More than 25 years ago my good friend Joan Mitchell suggested we do guided historical walks around the village: she would provide the organisation, and I would provide the historical information. These walks certainly proved popular, and they also showed an astonishing level of interest in our local heritage. Everyone, it seemed, had some tale to tell of old Newport. Before long we had organised our first Old Newport exhibition (in 1990), and this would be repeated in 1992, 1996 and 2005. We are now in the process of planning another for 2016. In 1990 I also felt it important to put in writing much of the information I had gathered, and so I produced the small book Newport's Story, out of print now for many years.

In the intervening years I have gathered so much more information about Newport's past and I now feel I should try to update that original Newport's Story, so that all the information I have been fortunate enough to unearth will not be lost. In 1890 William Neish wrote an excellent History of Newport. For me that book painted a picture of a Newport long gone, and brought it alive for me. I would love to think that a century from now this modest offering, whether in book form or in whatever electronic (or other) format it might then be available, might do the same for readers of the future.

I must also thank the many, many people in the village who know so much about Newport, and who have been kind enough to share some of their knowledge and memories with me. They have all contributed to Newport's story. I have certainly needed their help. After all I have lived here for only thirty four years, so am therefore still a relative newcomer. In the last few months a new Old Newport-on-Tay page on Facebook has created an astonishing amount of interest, with Old Newportonians the world over commenting on the photographs posted there, posting their own photographs in return, and relating their own stories and memories of Newport in the past. I've been thrilled with these responses and have loved every contribution to the page! It's good to think that this book might also bring back happy memories to all those who love Newport but who are now far removed from the village. Newport is such a wonderful place to live, and I'm sure this opinion was shared by the people who walked these streets and wandered along the shore, enjoying the sunsets and the wonderful vistas out over the river, long before we did.

Undoubtedly there is much of the village's history which I have not mentioned, but it is hoped that the information which is included will prove of interest to readers. Among these readers there will be many of you who already know a great deal about Newport, and perhaps you will forgive any unintentional omissions or errors. For those of you who read the book and have known little of the village's past beforehand, I hope you will enjoy learning something of Newport's history. If an interest in and enjoyment of the village's history are promoted through this book, then the book's main aim has been achieved.

Mairi Shiels
2016

CONTENTS

CONTENTS

This aerial view of the central area of the village in 1957 shows many changes. The Blyth Hall has no extension to the front, the old school is still in Blyth Street, and the Congregational Church at the bottom of Kilnburn is clearly seen. The granary is opposite the bottom of Cupar Road with the burgh yard next to it, and the old houses of Granary (Gas) Lane are still there as well as all the buildings to the rear of the Newport Hotel. J T Young's garage takes up most of Boat Road, and of course the ferry waits at the pier. The cars parked in Tayfield grounds have been left there by their owners as they visited the Royal Highland Show in Dundee.

EARLY DAYS

The development of the village of Newport as we know it today has taken place almost entirely over the last 200 years. Some ancient relics of earlier times have been found, but nothing to signify that any events of great importance ever took place locally. In 1865 for example, during excavations prior to the building of Westwood, now St. Serf's home, a number of burial urns containing human remains were uncovered. Whether these urns were, as was popularly believed at the time, associated with some earlier conflict or battle, or whether they just indicated the burial place of the early inhabitants of the district, has never been established. Some years earlier, close by, a stone sarcophagus containing bones had been found. Further east, on the ground above Northfield Farm, other remains were found in the 1830s. A stone coffin holding human remains was found within a stone cairn which was protected by earthworks. Again the date of these remains is unknown, although the 1855 Ordnance Survey map marks the spot as a "Site of Roman Camp (supposed)". The only certainty resulting from these finds is that this area has indeed been inhabited from early times. This is understandable, as the area would offer considerable advantages to early settlers. Large expanses of hill, valley and marsh would provide a wide range of hunting opportunities, while easy access to the River Tay provided not only fishing opportunity but also brought the shores of Angus within easy reach if necessary.

Early Ferries

There is no doubt that the most important factor in Newport's more recent development was the ferry crossing from here to Dundee. Originally there were four ferries crossing the Tay in this area, and they had operated for centuries. They were from Balmerino, Woodhaven and Seamills (the earlier name for Newport), all operating to Dundee, and from Ferryport-on-Craig (Tayport) to Broughty Ferry. All these ferries were still in regular use in the eighteenth century. There was great competition between them, especially between the ferries at Woodhaven and Seamills, which always tended to be the two most frequently used. Despite the importance of Woodhaven and Seamills, the ferries at Balmerino and Ferryport-on-Craig were nevertheless extremely important. Although the one at Balmerino was the first to stop operating as a ferry, in earlier times it had been much used especially when its abbey was inhabited. For much of the second

1

half of the nineteenth century and well into the twentieth, the pier at Balmerino was a popular stopping point for the pleasure steamers which plied up and down the river. A popular excursion was to take a steamer from Dundee to Balmerino, relax with some refreshment in the Balmerino Inn, before being carried by horse and carriage into Wormit and then returning to Dundee over the bridge by rail. The ferry from Ferryport-on-Craig crossed to Broughty Ferry. Ferryport-on-Craig is of course the old name for Tayport. When the railway company finally arrived in Tayport in the 1840s they decided that the old name was far too long and cumbersome for their timetables and station boards, and so the shorter name was adopted. The ferry from here was particularly popular with cattle drovers who appreciated the good pasturage available on both sides of the river.

The importance of the ferries at Seamills (Newport) and Woodhaven had long been recognised. They formed part of the great line of communication between the south and north-east of Scotland, and as early as 1669 an Act of Parliament had placed the ferries under the regulation of the Justices of the Peace of Fife and Forfarshire, who "should appoint fit and sufficient boats and convenient landing places". The two ferries enjoyed a healthy rivalry throughout the 18th century. In earlier times Woodhaven had tended to be more popular, although it is perhaps true to say that Seamills was potentially the more important, having the more navigable passage with fewer sandbanks to negotiate, and being nearer to Dundee. Certainly both ferries were well-used: by travellers to Dundee; by churchmen going to St. Andrews; by royal visitors from Falkland; and even by Rob Roy McGregor and his followers when escaping from a royalist army after a raid in Fife in 1715.

Seamills/Newport

Why the name "Seamills"? The name refers to meal mills which stood near the water here, near the area of the present pier. The only evidence of these mills today can be seen when looking up towards the burn tumbling down from the High Road. On the left is a large hole in the stone wall: this would have been the wall of the mill, and later the wall of the smiddy. The hole in the wall is where the water wheel was fixed, giving power first of all to the mill, and later to the smiddy. The water wheel was eventually removed in the 1940s. If present-day plans to develop this area and build houses come to fruition, then it will be even more difficult to imagine what this area, truly the historic heart of the village, was like so long ago. There were mills here for centuries, and it was in fact those

Early view of Boat road.
Old stone building beyond Young's cycle business was one of the original Sea mills.

mills which first gave Dundee an interest in the Fife side of the water, forging a strong link between the two places.

In the sixteenth and seventeenth centuries the Dundee corn mills could not cope with all the corn which the town was importing to feed its growing population. The magistrates therefore leased the mills at Seamills, on the Dundee Waterside, as the south bank of the Tay was then commonly known.

To meet the needs of the increased traffic between the two places, the Dundee Guildry in 1713 bought six acres of land around the Seamills from St. Fort (Sandford) and Inverdovat Estates. A new pier was built down below the old granary. The granary stood above the shore directly opposite the bottom of Cupar Road. It was a tall stone building with a flat-roofed area at the front, from which sacks of grain were carried by an aerial pulley to the waiting ships at the old pier. When the gasworks were started in 1865, the granary was then converted to housing for the workers. In its later years, most of the residents were becoming increasingly elderly: so much so that local children believed the name the Old Granary referred to the many old grannies living there! In 1961 the

3

The granary and old Dundee Guildry pier.

town council bought the granary for ten pounds. It was demolished in 1968 thus freeing land for the later Granary Lane housing development. All that remains today of the old pier are a few wooden stumps in the water, only visible at low tide. The Dundee Guildry also organised a more regular ferry service, and a house was built for the tacksman, or tenant, to be used as an inn and for horse-hiring. This building is long gone, but from 1840 onwards it would be used as Newport's first post office. It was then removed to make way in 1881 for Trinity Church. At this time of increased activity, the area on this side of the water began to be known as New Dundee, then Newport-Dundee and finally Newport. On Ainslie's map of 1775 for example, the name Newport-Dundee appears, but by the start of the nineteenth century the present day version appears to have been adopted.

The Dundee Guildry hoped to further develop the area commercially, so they then raised funds in Dundee and in other northern towns to make a road from Newport to Kirkcaldy, thus setting up a major route from Edinburgh to the north of Scotland via Newport. In doing this, the Dundee merchants hoped that such a route would lead to a flourishing new town on the Fife side, and thus a new outlet for Dundee traders.

Unfortunately for the Guildry

however the venture was a commercial failure, mainly, it would appear, as a result of bad planning and organisation. The Guildry were therefore relieved, around the 1770s, to sell the land and properties back to the original owners, St. Fort and

Inverdovat estates. This marked the end of Dundee's attempt to develop the area. However the legacy of Dundee's involvement in this side of the river was the new pier, the new inn and of course the new name!

Woodhaven

Throughout the eighteenth century the rivalry had continued between the adjacent ferries of Woodhaven and Newport. Woodhaven still tended to be more popular, despite the efforts of the Dundee Guildry, and would become even more so after 1790 when a new turnpike road was constructed from there to St. Michaels, connecting Woodhaven to St. Michaels and the road network

further south. This road followed the line of the present Flass road, and then continued up over the hill by Flass Farm. The very steep and lengthy inclines must have made this route quite a challenge for the horse-drawn carriages. In these early days it wasn't unknown for passengers to get out and help push the coach up the hill, and sometimes a 'cock-horse' was used: this was an

Woodhaven farm today.

extra horse hired to help up the steep hills. For several years however this new road certainly led to an increase in passenger numbers using the Woodhaven ferry. The toll-keeper's house at Woodhaven, beside the toll-bar, is now the site of the electricity sub-station. It was a two-storey building with an outside stair, with both a window at the side which looked down towards the pier and one to the front giving a view towards Flass, thus allowing the toll-keeper to watch for travellers from either direction. Next door was the Woodhaven Inn: later it became the home of the Mars captain and was known then as Mars Cottage, and is now a private house. The farm opposite had a brewery attached. The brewery produced strong ale and table beer, no doubt keeping the inn well supplied for thirsty travellers.

Apart from use by the passenger-carrying ferries, the harbours at Newport and Woodhaven were also used for exporting local produce such as corn, and for importing coal, wood and other necessities. Until the development of the nineteenth century railway system, trans-porting of goods was always so much simpler and cheaper by water, even where fairly lengthy and circuitous routes were used. The harbours at Newport and Woodhaven therefore provided essential services for the local area.

DEVELOPMENT OF ORGANISED FERRY SERVICES

As already indicated in the previous chapter, the early development of Newport resulted almost entirely from its suitability as a crossing point of the Tay estuary. The convenience of this crossing, and of course its close links with Dundee, had led to its first planned development around the pier area in the early 1700's. From these early beginnings an efficient ferry service developed which would serve communities on both sides of the river, and further afield, until the 1960s.

By the early 1800s the ferry services to both Newport and Woodhaven were thriving: in 1816 for example around 92,000 passengers used the Newport crossing. Altogether about twenty-five boats ran on the two passages, employing over one hundred men and boys. They were sailing boats: there were yawls, which were larger for animals and carriages, and which must have been extremely difficult to load, particularly with animals; and there were pinnaces, which were smaller, for passengers only, and which, with the right conditions, were faster than the steamships which would eventually replace them. The fare across the river was about 9d per head, but with the competition between Newport and Woodhaven, often only 4d or 6d was charged. (For the benefit of younger readers .... before the decimalisation of our coinage in 1971 there were twelve old pennies in a shilling, and twenty shillings in a pound. Old pennies were not 'p' but 'd'. 6d equals 2½p in our present coinage.) The ferries however were not very convenient: there were no set sailing times so they waited until they were full before departing. There was an unwritten rule among the ferrymen that boats waited until they had total fares to the value of four shillings and sixpence before leaving. This necessarily led to lengthy delays. Nor were they very safe. The passage was a treacherous one at the best of times, with the boats not perfectly suited to the crossing. The boats were frequently overcrowded and the crewmen not always sober. In addition, the passengers' confidence in the boats must have been severely tested when they saw some of the navigation methods in operation. For example, it's understood that a bale of straw was carried in the stern of the boat, and in foggy or misty weather lengths of straw were trailed over the back of the boat in the water. The direction that the straw took in the water apparently gave information to the boatmen about the strength, force and flow of the current and he could then plan his route accordingly.

Accident on the River

In general therefore, conditions were far from ideal, and matters came to a head in 1815 with a rather tragic occurrence: an accident out on the river, but one much less well known and documented than the much more famous one which would befall the rail bridge some sixty-four years later. The 1815 accident involved a pinnace travelling over from Dundee one Sunday morning in May, heading for Newport and well-filled with passengers. According to later accounts, it was over-filled with passengers. Most of these passengers were heading first to Newport, and from there to the village of Kilmany. They were going to church there, and they were willing to travel such a distance because they were going to hear Thomas Chalmers. Thomas Chalmers would later become Scotland's best-known preacher and in 1843 he would play the leading role in the Disruption and the formation of the Free Church of Scotland. His first charge was at Kilmany, and this particular Sunday morning would be his last sermon there before moving to Glasgow. His fame as a preacher had already spread and these travellers from Dundee were no doubt eagerly

looking forward to hearing him. Conditions on the river were not ideal that morning: there was a strong wind blowing from the south-east and it was meeting an ebb tide, making for very squally conditions. In addition, the captain of the pinnace decided to tow a yawl behind him. The outcome was that half-way across the river, the pinnace began to take in water and sank. The man on board the yawl did manage to rescue a few of the passengers but in fact 18 lives lost that morning.

The accident had been witnessed from Newport, and news of it spread very quickly. Indeed the minister of Forgan Kirk, the Rev Dr Maule, had to abandon his service completely, as his congregation grew ever more excited and distressed as word spread around the pews. Incidentally, the relief fund established to aid the bereaved families of the accident was used for the establishment of the Dundee Orphan Institution. The first children admitted to the new orphanage in Small's Wynd, Dundee were orphans from this disaster.

A Committee of Enquiry into the accident was set up, and this led to an Act of Parliament which authorised the erection of new piers on both sides of the river, and the procuring of better and safer boats. The Tay Ferry Trustees took over the running of the ferries in 1819 and one of their first acts was to appoint a superintendent at a salary of eighty pounds per annum with a free house. He immediately tried to arrange a more organised method of working the passage and various improvements were made. The number of operational boats was reduced to eight, with many of the older boats being sold by public roup in the Town Hall, Dundee. Crews were now carefully selected: in many cases the older men were pensioned off. In these cases compensation was paid for the loss of employment, certainly not normal practice in those days. Regular sailing times were set, and for the first time tickets were issued: a square ticket was issued if sailing from Dundee, and a round one from Newport. Generally arrangements were tightened up all round. Dogs were to be kept in a safe place on board, and no stallions were to be allowed on board except with the previous consent of owners of any horses already on board. These were wide-ranging improvements indeed! The improved conditions inspired a new confidence in the ferry, and traffic rapidly increased.

Introduction of Steam Ships

Perhaps the greatest improvement however came in 1821 when the first steamship, the Union, was introduced. It was built in Perth, but was fitted out with its engines by Carmichael Brothers of the Ward Foundry in Dundee. James and

The first steamship, the Union, at Newport pier in 1830s.
Tayfield House and Seamills Cottage, on the right, are the only buildings still existing.

Charles Carmichael would later become famous for producing Scotland's first locomotive engines in 1833 for the Dundee to Newtyle railway. The Union was a twin, or double-hulled, steamship with the paddle in the middle. Similar in style to ones already in use on estuarial crossings in America and on the Mersey, it seemed ideally suited to the Tay crossing. When pondering on the design of the new ferry, the Tay Ferry Trustees heard from a traveller of the success of twin-hulled ferries on New York's Hudson River, and they actually dispatched a local sea captain to America to investigate and to report back. A very positive report was received, but sadly the unfortunate captain very swiftly contracted typhus and died, so he never did return to the Tay to see his recommendation followed up. To begin with the Union sailed alternately to Woodhaven and to Newport. This however caused great confusion among travellers. In 1822 the Trustees decided that the two crossings were no longer necessary and so the Woodhaven service was discontinued. By this decision Newport's position as the most important crossing point on the river was therefore assured for the future.

The new thriving service from Newport led to a need for better facilities there, and so invitations were extended to two of the most eminent engineers of the day, Thomas Telford and Robert Stevenson. These two men were at the height of their engineering careers: Telford with a string of roads, bridges and canals to his name, and Stevenson the patriarch of the great lighthouse Stevenson family. They were asked to draw up plans for new piers and approaches for the ferry. Stevenson's plans were for a pier beside the existing one, while Telford's pier would be on an entirely new site further to the west. Telford's plans were adopted and in 1823 work started on the construction of a new pier and also on new roads to east and west. A new pier was also built at Dundee, (the Craig pier), and the new piers, combined with the improved steamboats, changed the crossing from one of the most dangerous in the country to one of the safest. The old Dundee Guildry pier continued to be used for commercial purposes until World War I, after which it gradually fell into disrepair. The stumps of this old pier can still be seen at low tide, at the bottom of Granary Lane.

Similarly at Woodhaven, the pier there continued to be used for commercial purposes after the ferry service was discontinued, and dues were paid to the St. Fort Estate. The owner, Mr Stewart of St Fort, had received compensation for the loss of revenue from the ferry. Unlike the old pier at Newport however, the

Woodhaven pier has continued to be used right up to the present day. For sixty years from 1869 until 1929 it was the landing place for the boys and officers of the Mars training ship, during World War II it was used by the Norwegian 333 Squadron and today it is still used by Wormit Boating Club. Further details of the Mars training ship and the activities of the Norwegians at Woodhaven can be found later in the book.

In 1823 the Union was joined by the George IV, again built in Perth and fitted with Carmichael engines. It was very similar to the Union but was slightly more powerful and had the addition of the first reversible engine in a steamboat. Together these boats provided a most regular service across the river, sailing every half-hour in both directions. Depending on the state of the tides the crossing usually took between fifteen and twenty minutes. Their period of operation was not without incident however. In an August gale of 1829, the Union broke down in the middle of the river. A rescue pinnace came out from Newport and ten passengers were safely transferred to shore, but four crewmen, all belonging to Newport, were lost during the transfer operation. The George IV was no less accident-prone: in 1824, while moored in Dundee, the ship caught fire, and had to be scuttled and sunk to avoid complete destruction. She was fully

repaired and sailed on until 1840.

As an indication of just how well-used the ferries were even in these early days of the steamers, the following figures make things clear: in 1824 the ships carried 100,536 passengers, 130 carriages, 474 gigs, 15,449 sheep, 4,777 horses and 2,563 loaded carts!

The Fifies

The Union and George IV were replaced by the Tayfield and the Princess Royal in 1836 and 1840 respectively, then very briefly in 1853, by the Newport (1). They in turn were replaced by the Fifeshire and the Forfarshire in 1858 and 1861, and the famous name Fifie stems from this time. The Fifeshire enjoyed great popularity and loyalty among the thousands of passengers who sailed on her every year. At 243 tons she dwarfed the previous Tay steamers, and had to lie idle for the first six months of her service on the river while the piers were altered to accommodate her. To begin with she was extremely accident prone. Within a few days of starting service in 1858 she bumped into the Craig pier in Dundee, dislodging masonry and damaging herself. In 1865 she broke down in a westerly gale, drifted downstream and passengers had to be landed at Tayport. In 1866 she collided in fog with a schooner in mid-stream. The following year, 1867, saw her run aground on the Dundee side with passengers being

The Fifeshire 1858-1929

landed by small boat. Even as late as 1920, one Sunday evening she broke down five minutes after leaving Newport. Many of the five hundred passengers on board were rowed back to Newport by Mars boys. Despite these mishaps, the Fifeshire steamed back and forward for an astonishing seventy-one years, developing a great reputation for reliability.

The Fifeshire and the Forfarshire were followed by the Dundee (1875) the Newport (2) (1910), Sir William High (1924) and B L Nairn (1929). These were all paddle-steamers. The Dundee made many pleasure cruises up and down the river, some of which proved to be quite eventful. In 1888 she struck a submerged breakwater at Newburgh, and eight hundred passengers had to be taken off. They were shocked later to see the Dundee half submerged. That same year, on an evening pleasure cruise the Dundee was narrowly missed by shells fired by Newport Artillery Volunteers practising on the beach! In 1919 the Dundee moved on to the River Forth where she worked the Queensferry passage until 1951, giving her a total service of seventy-six years. While working together on the Tay, the Fifeshire and the Dundee between 1875 and 1910 steamed nearly 500,000 miles each,

B L Nairn 1929-1966

carrying 750,000 passengers annually. Such exceptional service generated employment locally, both on board the ships and ashore. There was much loyalty among employees, and very often different generations of families were employed. The work however could be demanding and wages tended to be low. In 1912 for example the masters and engineers earned just forty shillings (£2) per week. Although at that time many families existed on considerably less than this, for such a skilled job it was not a particularly high wage even a century ago. Deck hands were paid just twenty-five shillings (£1.25) for a sixty-three hour week.

The William High and the B L Nairn were sister ships. Like the Newport and later the Scotscraig, they were built at the Caledon shipyard, Dundee. The B L Nairn was named after the Chairman of the Dundee Harbour Trust, and the William High after the Provost of Dundee from 1923-29. When he was knighted in 1929 then the ship too had to have a change of name to Sir William High. The period when these ships were operating, from the 1920s onwards, saw a tremendous increase in the number of motor vehicles using the ferries. Both ships had their deck layout altered to cope with the increase. Even after the last two ships, the Abercraig and the Scotscraig, were introduced, the B L Nairn continued in service as the relief vessel until the ferry service ended in 1966. The Sir William High was sold

The Abercraig 1939-1966

to a Nigerian company in 1953, and she was towed out to Lagos. She then steamed four hundred miles up the Niger River, was renamed Ojukwo and ended her days as a ferry on the Niger. She was not however the furthest travelled Fifie. After the Tayfield was taken out of service in 1853 she was sailed to Australia where she paddled up and down the Richmond River until being wrecked in 1859.

The last two boats, the Abercraig (1939) and Scotscraig (1951), were diesel-engined and much larger, and were designed for carrying a large number of cars. It was decided in the 1930s that the Abercraig would be fitted with German Voith-Schneider propellers, which would allow exceptional manoeuvrability in confined waters. Unfortunately by the time the Abercraig entered service in 1939, Britain was at war with Germany, and for the next few years servicing of the propellers by Voith-Schneider, or obtaining spares or even advice, was impossible. This was unfortunate, as they proved rather troublesome, and the ship was frequently out of service. Their advantages however outweighed the disadvantages, and it was decided to use Voith-Schneider again when the Scotscraig was being designed after the war. When this new ship, the last of the Fifies, was being built at the Caledon yard in Dundee, the new deck layout was drawn out on the quayside at the

The Scotscraig 1951-1966

Stannergate, allowing the designers to envisage the arrangement which would permit the maximum number of cars. After the launch of the Scotscraig in 1951, it was fortunate that the reliable work-horse B L Nairn was on hand as the relief boat. Time after time it was called into service: the Voith-Schneider propellers, which had proved so invaluable on other confined waterways, seemed to give nothing but trouble on the Tay. Interestingly the Scotscraig, costing £171,000, cost more than all the other steam ferries added together.

End of an Era
By the 1960s plans for the road bridge were well in hand, and the Abercraig and the Scotscraig, with the B L Nairn as relief boat, were in operation until the ferry service ended when the bridge was opened in 1966. During construction of the road bridge, there were frequent restrictions to the ferry service. As the bridge crept further out into the river, it blocked the route taken by ferries at low tide when they had to avoid the Middlebank sandbank. Sailings at low tide therefore had to be cancelled. The bridge did indeed prove to be an obstruction. On one occasion the Abercraig was driven by wind against the temporary bridge (the temporary bridge was a low level steel and wood structure allowing access and delivery of supplies to the actual bridge). Some

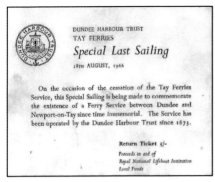

DUNDEE HARBOUR TRUST
TAY FERRIES

Special Last Sailing

18TH AUGUST, 1966

On the occasion of the cessation of the Tay Ferries Service, this Special Sailing is being made to commemorate the existence of a Ferry Service between Dundee and Newport-on-Tay since time immemorial. The Service has been operated by the Dundee Harbour Trust since 1873.

Return Ticket 5/-
Proceeds in aid of
Royal National Lifeboat Institution
Local Funds

Ticket for the last sailing on the Scotscraig.

damage was suffered by both the boat and bridge, and passengers had to be led to safety along the temporary bridge.

The final sailing of the Tay Ferries between Newport and Dundee took place on 18th August 1966 at 6 30 p.m. Earlier in the day the new Tay Road Bridge had been opened by Queen Elizabeth the Queen Mother and in the evening the Scotscraig made the final crossing. This event is remembered with great nostalgia by the ferry's regular travellers, and many people, both on board and on shore, photographed what was, without a doubt, the end of an era. As the Scotscraig left Newport for the last time it was packed with some 200 passengers who had willingly paid their five shillings for the historic return journey. On its return to Newport a service of thanksgiving for the Tay Ferries was held on the quayside.

With the end of the ferry service, the ships and the ferry piers were now redundant. Eventually the pier and

The Scotscraig in its other life as part of the Popeye film set in Malta.

buildings at Newport were taken over by Dundee University and used until 1997 as a marine research laboratory. Sadly the B L Nairn headed for the breaker's yard, and the Abercraig and Scotscraig headed for a new life in Malta. For some years they were used as pleasure vessels, until their usefulness in that capacity came to an end. The Scotscraig then ended its days, incredibly, as part of the 1980 Popeye film set. Half-sunk and realistically decorated with lush vegetation, for the purposes of the film she became a tropical island. That work done, she was towed into the Mediterranean and scuttled. The Abercraig languished for some years in a

Maltese harbour. Spotted there at various times by visiting Tayside holidaymakers, an attempt to save her and return her to Dundee came too late, and she was broken up and sold for scrap in 1995. The demise of the Abercraig in that Maltese harbour was the final conclusion to a long-lasting chapter of our Tayside history. However the Scotscraig has once again become a tourist attraction! Watch this amazing film https://www.youtube.com/watch?v= zDMbTmjgQqU which shows how in recent years the Scotscraig has become a popular site for escorted dives.

Management of the Ferries

From 1819 until 1843 the ferries had been managed by the Tay Ferry Trustees, and thereafter they were in the care of the Scottish Central Railway Company. This company had planned to carry a line from Glasgow and Stirling to Newport, and connect with Dundee by ferry, but the planned line did not in fact materialise. 1865 saw the amalgamation of the Scottish Central Railway Company with the much larger Caledonian Railway Company, and they therefore then briefly controlled the ferries. Within the next few years however the rival North British Railway Company was planning a railway bridge over the river, and in the face of such competition, by 1873 the Caledonian Railway Company was willing to sell the ferries to the Dundee Harbour

Trustees, who managed them until the service ended in August 1966. Unable to see into the future, and therefore unable to foresee the invention and monopoly of the motor car, the Caledonian Railway Company no doubt could not envisage a profitable future for the ferries after the railway bridge was built.

Management of the ferries by the Dundee Harbour Trustees was in general successful, with the ferries managing to pay their way. Nevertheless, their economic position was still rather fragile, especially after the opening of the second railway bridge in 1887. Fortunately for the ferries however, the development of the motor car would be their saviour. The huge increase in motor traffic in the new century underlined the continued need for vehicular transport over the river.

This huge increase in motor traffic at the beginning of the twentieth century required an improvement in the facilities at Newport pier. The pier was lengthened and broadened, and a low water landing stage was built, all of which would render much easier the loading and discharging of passengers and vehicles at all states of the tide. In addition a new waiting-room to accommodate up to four hundred people was added. A grand opening ceremony, presided over by Mr B L Nairn and Lord Provost William High, was held in 1928.

A busy ferry disembarks early 1900s.

Daily Exercise

The later Fifies all had a promenade deck above the saloon. Travelling in the saloon was slightly more expensive and many passengers preferred the bracing fresh air that went with the seat on deck to the stuffiness of the saloon. Indeed it was a common sight to see some businessmen having their daily exercise by walking round the deck. Frank Morrison, the first honorary burgess of Newport, declared that "the finest walk in Newport was on the deck of the Fifie". James Scrymgeour however recalled that it was a source of much amusement for youngsters, and very often giggling children were seen following and copying the adults. It has to be noted however that Newport residents were not always so keen on vigorous exercise. Many regular passengers who lived in the middle of Newport used a combined ferry and train season ticket for their daily commute to Dundee. This meant they could walk downhill to catch the ferry to Dundee in the morning, then return by train and walk home, again downhill, from the station.

Queueing for the ferry 1950s.

Weather

Such a vast, open estuary as the Tay can throw up the full spectrum of weather conditions. Fog was frequently a problem out on the river, making for a hazardous crossing and causing several accidents over the years. After World War II radar was fitted to the last four Fifies, much improving their safety. Prior to this, in foggy conditions, the Fifie would sound its siren as it crossed the river, until finally in reply would be heard the Newport pier bell. No doubt there would be a collective sigh of relief as the pier loomed into sight. In the most recent severely cold winter of 2010-2011 the people of Newport had a rare sight of the river almost covered in ice. In similar winter conditions in the past, when the upper stretches of the Tay were frozen over, the thaw would bring huge masses of ice down the river. As these enormous ice floes crashed against each other and piled up around the piers it became increasingly more difficult and dangerous for the ferry boats to make headway. In the icy winter of 1962-63 the Rev Robert Howieson described how only the old B L Nairn was able to keep going, and how adventurous it felt to stand out on deck and look down over her prow as she rammed her way through the ice.

Scotscraig approaching the pier.

Every winter the Fifies had to contend with strong gales funnelling down the firth. Strong winds seem to have become more frequent in recent years, and it appears that in the past, some years have had similar weather patterns. Apparently 1828-29 was an exceptional year, with regular storms causing great damage around the Tay estuary. On one occasion the Union was blown aground, on another occasion waves at Newport pier were thrown thirty to forty feet in the air, and a third storm washed away a large portion of the harbour wall in Dundee. Only in exceptionally rough weather however was the sailing actually cancelled. It's impossible to gauge whether the conditions which nowadays lead to the road bridge closures are any worse than those endured by the sturdy Fifies. It's interesting to note that after the building of the replacement railway bridge in 1887, passengers' confidence was slow to return, and in the stormiest of weather many reverted to the ferries, perceiving them to be safer.

Sadly, the ferries are now a distant memory for those who travelled on them: for too many others they are not even a memory. Many who now live on the south side of the Tay have never known the pleasure, excitement and sometimes the inconvenience of boarding a ferry to cross the river.

EARLY DEVELOPMENT OF THE VILLAGE

At the beginning of the nineteenth century, probably about twenty cottages made up the village of Newport. The population was between one and two hundred and most were boatmen or fishermen, and some tradesmen who provided necessary services for the small settlement. A fair proportion of the population was also involved in spinning and weaving: spinning was usually done by the women, hence the word 'spinster'; and weaving, much heavier work, by the men. The coarse brown linen cloth that was produced locally was called osnaburgh, a cloth that was originally imported from Osnabruck in Germany. Osnaburgh is also an alternative name for the village of Dairsie, and again relates to the weaving there of this particular cloth. There was salmon-fishing all along the river, and there is still evidence of this in the ice-house in Tentsmuir Forest and previously also at Tayport harbour. Also in Tentsmuir forest the march stone can be seen: this large upright slab of stone, dating from 1794, shows the boundary between the local salmon fishing districts of Shanwell and Old Muirs. Unfortunately the writing on the stone is becoming increasingly difficult to decipher with the passing years. In the Newport area the main salmon-fishing stations were at

A fine catch at the pier beach.

Woodhaven, and at Craighead, below the Tay Road Bridge. Salmon must have been plentiful in the river, as farm labourers on the Carse of Gowrie had it written into their feeing contracts that they did not want to eat salmon more often than twice each week! Fish caught were usually taken to Dundee to be sold in the market there, or sometimes packed in ice and taken on to London by Dundee steamships. At first the fishing was done by coble and rope nets, but after 1797 stake nets were used. So many fish were caught using this method however, and there was

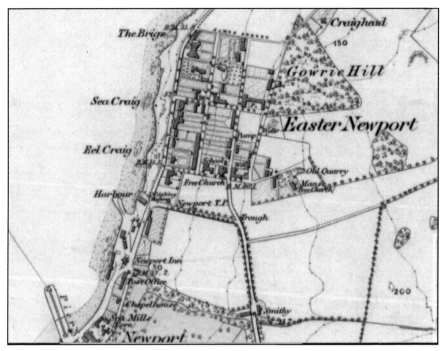

1855 map showing clearly the early development of Maryton (East Newport).

such an outcry from fishermen up-river, that those nets were banned after 1812. Agriculture and quarrying of whinstone were the only other forms of occupation at that time. The very hard whinstone produced locally would be used extensively in building throughout the nineteenth century as the village developed.

As the ferry service developed, so too did the village. At the end of the eighteenth century the estate of Tayfield came into existence. Before this most of the land which the village now covers formed part of the Barony of Inverdovat. In 1788 John Berry purchased most of

Inverdovat estate, built his house and named it Tayfield. His estate too soon took this name. Included in his purchases were the properties which had been put up by the Dundee Guildry during the period of their activity on this side of the river: the inn, the pier and various other buildings. Further details of Tayfield Estate come later in the book.

Cutting into the Tayfield land there was a large area, more or less from the lower end of Cupar Road as far as today's James Street, which belonged to the Scotscraig Estate at Tayport. In the early 1800s the village of Newport centred on the area around the pier and to the west, with little development in what we would now consider East Newport. As the community began to develop in the early nineteenth century, the owner of Scotscraig, Mr James Dalgleish, decided to found a new village east of Cupar Road as a rival to Newport proper. So he feued the land, and called the village Maryton after his wife. William Street, Robert Street and James Street were named after his three sons. Many of the feus were quickly taken up and the village experienced its first spurt of growth. This early development can be seen very clearly on the 1855 Ordnance Survey map: it was very much a planned development with its straight streets criss-crossing at right angles.

The more efficient ferry services were of course the main reason for this initial growth, and the benefits of the ferries are illustrated in a "Fife Herald" advertisement from 1823 for a piece of Mr. Dalgleish's land.

Fife Herald   1823

"What must render this ground so peculiarly adapted for a country residence and bathing quarters to families generally resident in Dundee, is its contiguity to the public ferry........The boat......will convey passengers across the river in twelve minutes.......without any fatigue whatsoever."

The ferries also determined the type of village Newport would become. By the middle of the century, Newport was becoming a dormitory suburb of Dundee, and a very convenient holiday resort for Dundee's businessmen. Many families would come over to stay for a month or two in the summer, while husband or father could easily travel back over the river on a daily basis for business in Dundee.

Coaching Days

Also contributing to the village's development at this time was the coaching activity. The turnpike road to Woodhaven (1790) has already been mentioned. Turnpike roads could be built in an area after a Turnpike Act for that area had been passed in Parliament. The first Turnpike Act relating to this area of Fife was passed in 1790. The building of the roads was organised by a group of Turnpike Trustees, who were usually local land-owners and any other interested and influential parties. Turnpike roads were, in general, a great improvement on the previous ones. Tolls were paid and the money raised was used for the maintenance of the roads. These toll charges would be displayed on large highly-visible boards.

In 1808, a turnpike road was built into Newport. To a great extent, this was thanks to the efforts of John and William Berry of Tayfield, who

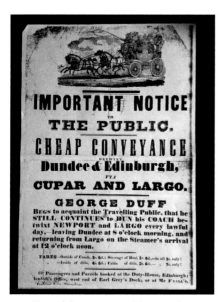

One of the many coaching services through Newport.

Cupar Road. The toll-house and toll-gate were demolished at the end of the nineteenth century to allow the building of Robertson Place, the row of shops from 1-19 Cupar Road. The immediate result of the building of the new road was an increase in coaching traffic and passengers using the ferry and other facilities in Newport. In 1806 John and William Berry had the Newport Inn built, replacing the one put up by the Dundee Guildry, and it was ready to take full advantage of the increase in coaching activity which resulted from the new road. Until the 1820s it was of course the old pier down behind the High Street which was still in use. The hotel was therefore very conveniently situated. Even after the new pier was built, the old one continued to be used for commercial purposes until the start of the twentieth century. The old pier belonged to Tayfield, and the estate office, immediately opposite the hotel, was well positioned to monitor the comings and goings at the old pier.

arranged for a mile of the road to be built on their land. They had realised the tremendous benefits to their own properties (inn, granary and pier) and indeed to the whole village that such a road would bring. The construction of the road linked Newport by a good road system to Cupar and the Pettycur Ferry. This ferry operated just south of Kirkcaldy, and was at that time the most important crossing point on the Forth. It was also the ferry used by most coaches travelling north through Fife. The building of Newport's turnpike road, and its connection to Pettycur, immediately removed Woodhaven's advantage over Newport. The toll gate for this new road stood just at the bottom of

A new road running east-west linking Newport to Woodhaven and Tayport was completed in 1830, seven years after work on the new pier had begun. The Newport-Tayport stretch of this road was taken over by the Turnpike Trusts in 1835. The toll-gate and house for this latter stretch of road were on the Tayport road beyond Northfield farm.

Newport milestone.

The stage-coaches passing through Newport at this time would normally be pulled by two, four or six horses. The coaches might carry six passengers inside, and up to twelve outside. Travelling 'outside' was of course much cheaper, but passengers had to put up with the danger of falling off, discomfort and the weather. There would also be the coachman, sometimes a guard, and luggage and parcels. With this heavy load to pull, the horses managed about eight-ten miles per hour. Journeys were divided into 'stages' of perhaps eight or ten miles. The guard would warn the next staging-inn to have fresh horses ready for their arrival, by blowing loud and long on his horn – his 'yard of tin'. Royal Mail coaches were the stars of

the road. They were easily recognised in their scarlet, black and gold paint. The crack driver and armed guard were dressed in scarlet and black Post Office uniform. Nothing was allowed to delay a Royal Mail coach. The guard's horn warned not only the inns, but also the toll-keepers to have the toll-gates open: mail coaches travelled toll-free. Their main purpose was to carry the mails, and the guard would guard these with, if necessary, his life. Passengers were happy to pay a little extra for the privilege of travelling in these efficient vehicles.

By 1840 coaches from Edinburgh to the north, from Aberdeen to the south, from St Andrews to Dundee, and between Cupar and Dundee were all passing through Newport. The Royal Union, the Defiance, the Earl of Strathmore, the Kingdom of Fife, the Thane of Fife and the Tallyho were just some of the romantically-named coaches to be seen in the village. Sadly, it was one of these, the Kingdom of Fife, which was involved in Newport's only fatal coaching accident. In 1836, a Mr Alexander Kidd of Newport tried to alight from the coach as it was still moving down Cupar Road, and was run over by the coach wheels.

With all this coaching activity, for much of the first half of the nineteenth century Newport experienced a real coaching heyday. It's difficult to imagine now what a booming, bustling, noisy place it must have been, with frequent coaches rolling in from the south, horses being changed with all the attendant noise and excitement, ferries arriving and departing, and passengers refreshing themselves or just stretching their legs before the next stage of their journeys.

However the coaching heyday ended for Newport in 1848 when a branch railway line was built from Leuchars to Tayport. The widespread enthusiasm for this new form of transport meant that from then on many travellers heading north preferred to take the train to Tayport, continuing from there by ferry to Broughty Ferry, thus bypassing Newport altogether. This route became even more popular after 1851, because in that year the world's second train ferry, the Robert Napier, was introduced on the crossing. This remarkable piece of engineering carried whole trains across the river, from specially constructed piers at Broughty Ferry and Tayport. It was designed by railway engineer Thomas Bouch, already a railway engineer of some renown, and later better known for his ill-fated first Tay railway bridge. The world's first train ferry, the Leviathan, also designed by Thomas Bouch, had operated successfully on the Forth between Granton and Burntisland since the previous year. The train ferry between Tayport and Broughty Ferry was therefore the final link in the chain of the North British Railway Company's route between Edinburgh and Dundee. Although bringing enormous economic benefits to Tayport, the arrival of the railway there meant the opposite for Newport. Newport would now be bypassed, and so ended quite suddenly the village's first phase of development.

THE COMING OF THE RAILWAY

The next major factor contributing to the growth of the village was the building of the railway bridge. The Leuchars-Tayport rail link of 1848 had a delaying effect on Newport's development which lasted approximately twenty years until work started in 1871 on the new bridge.

The idea of a bridge was not new. As early as 1842 plans had been drawn up for a floating bridge, or chain ferry, from Craighead to Dundee, which would follow almost the same line as the present-day road bridge. Although this floating bridge may well have provided a more efficient service than the existing ferry service, the plans came to nothing. Instead the idea of a railway bridge was soon being considered.

In the mid-nineteenth century two great railway companies, the Caledonian and the North British, battled for supremacy on the Scottish railway scene. Passengers travelling to the north-east had a choice. They could travel with the Caledonian railway on a slightly circuitous route from Edinburgh via Stirling, Perth and Dundee. The alternative was shorter and much more adventurous: the North British railway would carry them across the Forth and Tay estuaries on Thomas Bouch's train ferries (see end of previous chapter). Given the right

conditions this route was shorter in time as well as in distance, but it was subject to the vagaries of tides and weather and unfortunately passengers very often had to endure the discomfort of sea-sickness – not exactly what was expected when embarking on a train journey. Most passengers therefore tended to opt for the more predictable, if longer, Caledonian route.

Plans for a Railway Bridge

By the 1860s the North British directors were coming to the conclusion that if they were ever to offer a permanently more attractive service than their rivals the Caledonian could, then both estuaries on the North British route would have to be bridged. Thus an idea which had existed before this time in the minds of some men as just a dream, would now become a reality. Thomas Bouch, one of the men who had long held that apparently impossible dream, was the man charged with the task of designing and building bridges over both the Forth and the Tay. He would start with his bridge over the Tay.

The decision to build a bridge over the Tay would have huge implications for Newport. After looking at various alternatives it was decided that the bridge should cross from Wormit Bay to Magdalen

First bridge under construction with Wormit foundry in foreground.

Green. A connecting line would run from the bridge to Leuchars via a new station at St Fort. More importantly for Newport however, the bridge would be linked to Tayport via two new stations at Newport: Newport East and Newport West. When the first railway bridge was built there was no station provided at Wormit. The village did not develop until after the bridge was built and so the provision of a station there was not considered necessary. It was only when the replacement bridge was built that Wormit had its station.

The Wormit Bay crossing was selected after test bores on the river bed showed that under the initial layers of sand and gravel, there was a firm layer of rock apparently stretching almost entirely across to Dundee. Bouch's design was for a slender single-track bridge, with 89 horizontal lattice iron-work girders, supported on solid brick pillars. To maximise the height above the river for shipping heading to and from Perth, the fourteen central girders would be built up higher.

Work on the bridge commenced at Wormit Bay in July 1871 and soon the structure was creeping out into the river. Complications however arose during construction when it was discovered that, contrary to pre-building reports, the bed of rock, thought to extend all the way across the river, did not do so. This had been considered essential to provide a firm foundation for the bridge pillars. It was therefore back to the drawing board for Bouch, and he decided to change the design of the remaining pillars and use lattice iron columns instead of brick ones. These would be lighter and would put less pressure on their bases. The lattice iron work would also offer less resistance to wind and so it could be argued that the bridge would be more stable. He also reduced the number of pillars, which of course necessitated lengthening some of the girders. Work therefore continued to this new design. Inevitably this alteration to design would require a considerable increase in ironwork on the bridge. Accordingly a foundry was established at Wormit to allow the new columns to be made there. The foundry was just to the east of the bridge, on the high ground above the river.

The Bridge in Operation

After seven years of construction the bridge was finally ready for passenger use in May 1878. This was after it had been passed as safe and suitable by Board of Trade inspectors. The board inspection had been fairly rigorous, but strangely had not included any tests to assess the bridge's strength under great wind pressure. The only recommendation by the inspectors was that trains should not exceed 25mph when crossing. The bridge was hailed as the technological wonder of the age and it certainly fulfilled all the hopes of the North British

directors. A sure sign of its success came the following summer when Queen Victoria crossed the bridge in the royal train on her journey south from Balmoral. Soon the North British was carrying eighty-four per cent of rail traffic between Edinburgh and Dundee, traffic between Dundee and Fife had more than doubled, passenger travel times were cut considerably and goods traffic increased beyond all expectations. The bridge formed a most important link in the east coast route, and a future Forth Bridge would ensure the prosperity of all north-east towns as well as the profits of the North British Railway Company.

Despite the clear benefits of the bridge in these first months, there were nevertheless some concerns being expressed. Some passengers were uneasy at the speed of trains using the bridge, which frequently appeared to be in excess of the stipulated 25mph. This was especially noticeable in the mornings when the trains were said to race the ferries from Newport to Dundee, no doubt enthusiastically encouraged by their respective passengers. William Robertson of Balmore, Newport, watched from his house and timed the trains passing through the High Girders. He was so concerned by his findings that he abandoned his railway season ticket altogether and reverted to using the ferries. Another

The first bridge completed.

Newport resident, John Leng, owner of the Dundee Advertiser, complained of a curious prancing motion as the carriages passed over the bridge. Of course some maintenance was done on the bridge, but in fact Henry Noble, the man responsible for maintenance on this lattice iron structure, was qualified not in iron-work but in brick-work. His maintenance crew was also cut down quite early on from seven men to just three. Finally, painters working on the bridge were concerned to see large numbers of iron bolts lying about, many of which they saw falling out of the spans as trains crossed over. It appears that little was done to address any of these concerns as they were raised.

The opening of the connecting Newport railway one year later in May 1879 was a rather low-key affair, with no official ceremony to mark the occasion, only the explosion of a few fog signals on the arrival of the first train from Tayport at the Tay Bridge station in Dundee. But the railway's impact on Newport would be immense, and once again Newport was linked to the rest of the country by a modern transport system.

Apart from improved communications, the new bridge provided another benefit for the people of Newport and area: a new water supply. By the 1870s the benefits to health of a pure water supply were becoming apparent, and government legislation was pressurising local authorities to improve sanitation generally in their areas. In Newport many of the private wells in the village had been found to be impure, and the rapid population growth necessitated a new water supply. The Forgan parish board considered plans to implement a local water supply, using water gathered in the hills behind the village, but the cost of the necessary pipe work and construction of two storage reservoirs would have been around £25,000. Much cheaper, at just £7,000, and indeed probably more efficient, would be to bring water from Dundee's new supply at Lintrathen over the railway bridge. The board's decision was eventually hastened by a fairly disastrous fire in one of the new High Street shops. The fire rapidly spread to adjoining shops and to the houses above, and was not brought under control until twenty men of the Dundee Fire Brigade eventually arrived by ferry, bringing appropriate fire-fighting equipment with them. Had a sufficient water supply been available, the fire might well have been contained sooner. The decision was now made, and Dundee Water Commissioners laid a pipe over the bridge and built a reservoir on Wormit Hill. By November 1879 the new water supply was flowing through the village; none of the residents dreamed that in just over a month it would be cut off again most suddenly and unexpectedly.

The Great Storm
The Tay Bridge disaster of Sunday 28th December 1879 is well documented history. According to contemporary reports the storm which hit Tayside and the rest of Scotland that evening was quite awesome in its ferocity, with dozens of incidents of serious structural damage being experienced across Dundee. Out on the river, on the training ship Mars, Captain Scott estimated that the gale coming down the firth was between forces 10 and 11 on the Beaufort scale, a strength very rarely experienced. Struggling through that storm, battling its way towards the Tay Bridge, came the 5.20 train from Burntisland. No doubt any passengers on the train who had come all the way from Edinburgh, and who would therefore have already crossed one turbulent stretch of water in a storm-tossed ferry boat, would be thankful that the next estuary would be crossed in the relative comfort of their railway carriage on the wonderful new Tay Bridge.

At St Fort station, the last before the bridge, tickets were collected from the passengers. The train then passed the Wormit signal box at the south end of the bridge, before trundling out onto the bridge and disappearing into the darkness.

It is probably true to say that no-one actually saw the Tay Bridge fall. It would appear that the weather

Artist's impression of the disaster from the Illustrated London News.

conditions made for such complete darkness at the time of the accident that it was impossible for anyone on either shore to see what actually happened. There were however several eye-witness accounts which clearly described seeing two or three flashes, and others which noted a towering column of spray rising high in the air. Out on the Mars training ship, the deck watchman probably had the clearest view. He was watching the lights of the train flicker as it entered the high girders. At that moment a great gust of wind caught the ship, presumably the very gust that toppled the bridge, and he turned for cover. When he looked again the flickering train

lights had disappeared, and so too had the central spans of the bridge. News of the disaster spread quickly on both sides of the river. That Sunday evening, despite the weather, crowds began to gather along the waterfront. Distraught relatives of possible passengers on the train converged at Tay Bridge station, desperate to know more. At first little could be done to gain any further information. Owing to the dreadful weather it was some hours before any ship could try to approach the bridge. Eventually at ten o'clock the ferry Dundee, which normally operated on the Newport-Dundee crossing, managed to get close to the scene and those aboard were able to make out the full extent of the damage. Although there was much debris floating about, there was no sign at all of any bodies, and certainly not of any survivors. First estimates of the scale of the disaster were actually much worse than the reality. Early news reports, using information given by railway officials, put the possible list of casualties at 300. A more accurate figure was later reached by the simple act of counting the tickets taken from the passengers at St Fort station. For many years the accepted number of casualties has been 75. However more recently Murray Nicoll of Dundee has done extensive research on the subject and can find evidence of no more than 59. There is still some doubt about the final total and this would therefore be a minimum figure. Memorials recently erected (28th December 2013) on both sides of the river at Dundee Riverside and Wormit Bay, list the names of the fifty-nine known casualties.

The Aftermath

The search for bodies and wreckage got under way the next morning. The first body, that of a Miss Annie Cruickshank, was washed up on the shore at Newport later that day, but the search for the others would be a long slow process, taking many weeks. Indeed at one point the services of a clairvoyant were called in to give more unconventional guidance on where the bodies might be located. Among the hundreds of men involved in the search were local fishermen, mussel-dredgers and many of the Dundee whalers, who were well used to working in such cold and hostile conditions. It is doubtful however whether they were all motivated entirely on compassionate grounds; perhaps the reward offer made by the North British railway company of five pounds for each body recovered may have spurred many of them into action. In the end only forty-six bodies were recovered, the last-but-one being found nearly four months after the disaster in the far north of Scotland near Wick.

There was much more success in locating wreckage and eventually the whole train was found, still contained within the high girders down on the river bed. When the engine was recovered, it was laid up for some weeks on the shore at Tayport, no doubt providing an opportunity for local lads to scramble over it, acting out their engine-driver fantasies. It was then removed to Glasgow for repairs costing just £50, a remarkably small amount even in those days and surely a great tribute to her original Scottish builders. The engine was soon back on the rails, and steamed on for another astonishing 40 years, affectionately known throughout that time by her drivers as the "Diver". The carriages were of

The calm after the storm.

course of much flimsier construction, and had suffered considerable damage. No personal effects, or bodies, were found in any of the carriages, clearly an indication of just how swift the current was out on the river that night and in the succeeding days.

Court of Inquiry

A Court of Inquiry into the accident was very quickly set up, and it first met in January 1880 in Dundee. Throughout its proceedings the inquiry attracted enormous public interest, and a report on the disaster was finally presented in June. During the inquiry one hundred and twenty witnesses had given answers to almost twenty thousand questions, and it is only possible here to give a very brief summary of the evidence presented.

Much disturbing evidence had come to light during the inquiry. William Robertson of Newport, who had timed the trains as they crossed the bridge, had estimated the speed of one train to be as much as 42 mph. The North British Railway Company was prepared for this accusation of speeding, and the reliable drivers questioned of course denied that they ever exceeded the speed limit. It did however seem to be an accepted fact that very often the early morning trains from Newport to Dundee did race the ferry boats across the river.

Even more disturbing was the evidence from the workers at the Wormit foundry. It appeared that the iron columns of the bridge had been made from a low grade iron which varied in thickness from half an inch to the required inch thickness. When the iron columns were cast, they were sometimes faulty, with holes in them. These holes had often been filled with an iron paste called Beaumont's Egg, and they had then been sent out on the river to be used on the bridge. The use of Beaumont's Egg for repairs was in fact fairly common practice in foundry work, but not when the finished article would come under any great stress, so it should certainly not have been used on the columns of the Tay Bridge. Each of these columns was made from six sections bolted together in a hexagonal structure, and further concerns were heard about the bolt holes. These should have been cylindrical and tight-fitting, but in fact many seemed to be conical and therefore quite loose fitting. This probably explains why so many bolts worked loose.

During the period when the bridge was in operation, maintenance of the bridge was in the hands of Mr. Henry Noble. During this time no other inspection of the bridge by any other officials was made, and at no time was Mr. Noble given instructions on what maintenance should be carried out. Mr Noble appears to have been most diligent, but, as already mentioned, his maintenance crew of seven men was soon reduced to just three, and his own qualifications for the job were sadly inappropriate. This man, who had the responsibility for the longest, greatest railway bridge in the world, a bridge made almost entirely of latticed iron work, was qualified not in iron-work, but in brick- and stone-work. And when he found long, narrow slits in the iron-work of some of the columns, and cracks in the masonry of twelve of the piers, and reported them to Thomas Bouch, he was told to strap them up with bands of iron as that should be sufficient repair.

The Inquiry also heard evidence from the Astronomer Royal and a Professor of Mathematics from Cambridge University. They both gave very detailed evidence on the effects of wind speed and pressure, suggesting that not enough account of these had been taken during the planning and building of the bridge. Finally it was the turn of Sir Thomas Bouch himself to give evidence. It appeared that throughout the whole procedure of planning, building and maintaining the bridge he had relied and depended too heavily on information and advice from others. When designing the bridge he had relied completely on information given to him on the rock formations in the river and on the effect of wind speed and pressure, during construction he had believed absolutely in the quality of work being carried out at the Wormit foundry and during the bridge's short life he had complete faith in Mr. Noble's skills and abilities as a bridge inspector.

The conclusion of the report found that the bridge had been "badly built, badly constructed and badly maintained"; furthermore, it laid the blame for the disaster almost entirely on Thomas Bouch. The conclusion found that:

For faults in design –
he was entirely responsible.
For faults in construction –
he was principally responsible.
For faults in maintenance –
he was principally, if not entirely, responsible.

This was a harsh verdict on a man who had simply built his dream, and it was a verdict that broke his heart and spirit. With nothing more to live for, Sir Thomas Bouch died just three months later, aged 58. He had been destroyed by the destruction of his bridge and, indeed, as John Prebble has suggested, he was perhaps the last casualty of the Tay Bridge Disaster.

The Replacement Bridge

There's no doubt that the fall of the Tay Bridge was a huge drawback to the people on the south side of the river who, in the short period of the

Rebuilding – the difference between the old and the new.

bridge's operation, had become used to the convenience of 'taking the train'. This would be particularly the case for those of Dundee's middle classes who had taken advantage of the bridge to move over permanently to the south side of the river. However, the bridge collapse probably caused more inconvenience to the people of Newport and Wormit by the loss of their fine new water supply than by the loss of railway communications: after all they still had the ferries. Until the new bridge was built, the stream at Wormit Bay was brought into use, and the water was pumped from there up to the new reservoir on Wormit Hill. This maintained the water supply until 1887 when the

Wormit station and the new bridge.
Note the nearby carpet-beating works.

replacement bridge opened.
The decision to rebuild the bridge was made almost immediately following the disaster. The enormous success of the first bridge whilst in operation made the decision to rebuild almost a foregone conclusion. The task of redesign was given into the capable hands of engineer William Barlow.

Plans for the new bridge had to take several factors into consideration. First of all, was the present site the most suitable or was there a better one? Secondly, navigational interests had to be considered, and thirdly, and surely the most important, there must be no doubt about the new bridge's safety.

Barlow threw himself enthusiastically into the task ahead of him. Extensive tests and experiments were carried out on the river bed to ascertain whether or not it could support a more substantial bridge. Once reassured on this point, Barlow produced a design for a double track bridge to be built eighteen metres upstream from, and parallel to, the previous bridge. More substantial foundations and piers and a reduction in height would ensure the new bridge's stability under great wind pressure.

It was decided that the bridge should be built By William Arrol and Company, an engineering firm with an excellent pedigree in iron

A very early view of East Newport station.

Goods train leaving East Newport.

Full steam ahead for Tayport, pictured behind Craighead Road.

1960s and a diesel at East Newport.

bridge construction. The foundation stone was laid on July 6th 1883 and throughout construction thorough checks were carried out on the structure's strength and safety. The girders on the remaining sections of the old bridge were undamaged and, as a measure of economy, they were transferred for use on the new. The piers of the original were retained as breakwaters, offering protection to the new piers from the scouring effects of tides and currents. They are still clearly visible, poignant reminders of that long-ago tragedy.

The opening of the new bridge in July 1887 restored both railway communications and the all-important water supply to the village. From then until the 1960s the railway and ferries together provided Wormit, Newport and Tayport with an efficient, integrated transport system.

In 1966 when the new dual carriageway to the road bridge was being constructed, it was decided to close the line to Tayport to save building an underpass where the two routes crossed. Passengers were taken on to Tayport by bus. The Newport line and stations survived a further three years after the opening of the road bridge before the last train ran on 5th May 1969.

The Railway Today

There is still much of the railway and its infrastructure to be seen between Newport and Wormit. Most of the route of the old railway line has been converted to cycle path and public pathway, all forming parts of the local nature trail, and it possible to walk from Wormit to Tayport, for much of the way on the old rail route. The station building at East Newport has been converted to a house, but it is easily recognisable, still with its neat white station fence. There is very little evidence of the

West Newport station, but there is an excellent information board nearby, at the top of Kinbrae Park, recently erected by the community council. Wormit station, situated immediately at the south end of the bridge, was dismantled and can still be visited, although a little further afield. It now plays a new role as station building at the Bo'ness steam preservation railway station. Very close to where the station stood are the entrances to two tunnels, one used by the line from the first bridge and one by the line from the replacement bridge. Another information board above the bridge landfall gives the background to the Tay Bridge Disaster.

As the railway passed through the grounds of Tayfield Estate it was carried over the 'den' on a substantial viaduct. It is interesting to note that originally the viaduct columns were made of latticed ironwork and were similar in design to those on the first railway bridge. According to Jim Smith, when a crack opened in one column, immediate preventive measures were taken. The viaduct was closed for nine months and the columns were encased with brick and filled with concrete. If this is true, then lessons had indeed been learned from the 1879 disaster. Although the viaduct was removed after the closure of the railway in 1969, the supports can still be seen today. (Jim Smith was born and lived on the

Tayfield Estate with his family. His father had come there in 1927 as a forester. Jim grew up there, then worked first as a forester and eventually as estate overseer.)

Accidents at Wormit

The 1955 rail crash at Wormit. White clad tennis players rushed to help.

The tunnel at Wormit was unfortunately the scene of several accidents over the years. On entry to the tunnel the railway line made a sharp turn before heading east towards Newport. On several occasions trains appeared to be travelling too fast to accommodate the turn. The worst accident occurred in May 1955 when a Dundee-bound train derailed as it emerged from the tunnel. On board the train were hundreds of Dundee children returning home from Sundayschool picnics at Windmill Park in Newport and at Tayport Common., There were three fatalities, all of whom were on the footplate of the engine: the fireman, a young boy and an adult passenger. More than forty passengers were injured, some seriously. Nearby tennis players and local residents rushed to help and it's gratifying to learn that their efforts were later commended in parliament by the Minister for Transport. The ensuing Committee of Enquiry found driver error and excessive speed to be the main causes of the accident. Less

41

serious was an accident in 1931 when an early morning train from Tayport jumped the points at Wormit station. The engine mounted the platform, destroying a good section of it, and the first carriage derailed. The station was busy at the time with would-be passengers heading for school and work, and it was therefore a miracle that no-one was seriously injured.

The Delights of the Newport Railway

William McGonagall was well aware of the charms of the railway line on the south shore of the Tay, and was full of praise in his poem The Newport Railway. For ninety years the route from Tayport to Wormit must have rated as one of the great short railway journeys, offering a delightful variety of scenes and scenery all packed into a few short miles. Any model railway enthusiast intent on creating an ideal rail layout would do well to copy some features from this route. Starting right beside the harbour in Tayport, the train chugged steadily up the incline to Newport. After leaving Tayport, the fields and open countryside offered splendid views of Broughty Ferry with its castle guarding the entrance to the estuary, and of Dundee harbour and all the related shipping activity on the river. Soon the train was passing the elegant villas of Newport and the lush vegetation and woodland of Tayfield Estate.

The viaduct there and the tunnel at Wormit illustrated the fine engineering skills of the Victorian builders. Stops at Newport East and Newport West allowed the passenger to admire the neat and tidy stations, particularly at Newport West where the burnished brasses, hanging baskets and beautiful floral displays frequently resulted in the station winning awards in the 'best-kept station' competition. And of course, throughout the whole journey, but especially as the train gained the high ground from Newport to Wormit, there were these magnificent vistas, never the same on any two days, out over the river to the Dundee skyline and beyond to the mountains of Angus and Perthshire.

East Newport station.

West Newport station.

FURTHER DEVELOPMENT OF THE VILLAGE

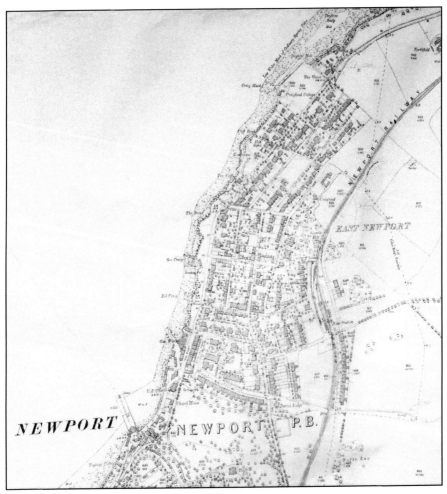

East Newport 1894.

The improvement in communications resulting from the railway's arrival speeded up the feuing of Newport, and it was from the 1860s onwards, when the idea of a bridge and a connecting line through the village was becoming a real possibility, that the village experienced its second major period of expansion. It was at this time that

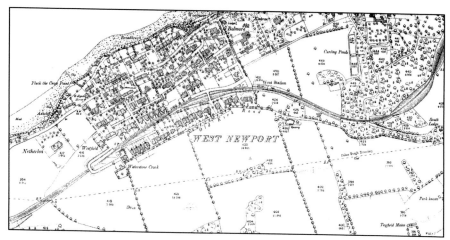

West Newport 1894.

many of the most elegant private villas were built, in the terrace pattern familiar today in both East and West Newport and eventually in Wormit also. Whereas earlier in the century Dundee families might only have come to stay in Newport for the summer months, now many business and professional men chose to move over here permanently, enjoying the purer air, the fine sea bathing and the lower rates which the area offered. The Ordnance Survey map of 1897 shows this development very clearly. This development is also illustrated by the population figures. Between 1841 and 1861 the population increased very slowly from 584 to 719. Just ten years later in 1871 it had more than doubled to 1507, with another huge increase to 2311 by 1881. The greatest increase was in East Newport.

Much of the land feued in East Newport at this time belonged to the Tayfield Estate, especially to the east of James Street. Part of that area became known as 'the Bank', as the man who took over this land fell into financial difficulties, and the feus were taken over by the Clydesdale Bank – hence the name Bank Street. One piece of ground in this area was not built on until after the Second World War. The rectangle between Kerr Street (previously named Woodriffe Terrace) and Tay Terrace belonged to Craighead Farm and as such could not be built upon. Craighead Farm itself disappeared in the post-war building of Craighead Road and Elizabeth Crescent, and the field below suffered a similar fate. Immediately after the war, the site was used for pre-fabs. These were pre-fabricated houses which could be built in a day

45

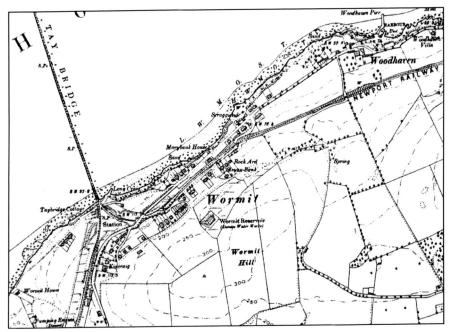

Wormit 1894.

and were the government answer to the post war housing shortage. Although built quickly and with a limited life expectancy, the pre-fabs had all mod cons and were much loved by their occupiers. Indeed there was a thriving little social network there with the residents running beetle drives and such like. The pre-fabs would later be replaced by the more modern 1970s houses still there.

At the time of the erection of the first railway bridge the lands of Wormit and beyond were owned by the Wedderburns of Birkhill. Mr Wedderburn anticipated that the bridge construction would lead to a flurry of house building in the area.

Accordingly he feued land around Wormit Bay, imagining a thriving village taking shape there. A concrete sea wall was built and a terrace walk was laid out to provide a pleasant promenade for the residents in the imagined village. Hopes for this development were dashed by the fall of the bridge. Only Wormit House was built as part of this ambitious scheme, but almost 150 years later, we can still enjoy that terraced walkway.

Gasworks and Electricity
In 1856 a Gas company was formed in Newport and most of the shares were quickly purchased. Gasworks were erected between the High

View of pier and village. Gas works chimney clearly seen.

Street and the river, to the south-west of the old harbour and close to the granary, and soon coal gas was replacing oil and candles in most of the houses in the village. In early photographs the tall chimney immediately behind the High Street shops shows the position of the gasworks. The price of gas to customers was fairly high, certainly higher than in Dundee, but the gas did appear to be of an excellent quality. Fire damaged part of the gasworks in 1903, and they were replaced by new ones just outside the village on the Tayport road: these were administered by the new town council. Meanwhile the site of the old gasworks became the burgh yard until local government re-organisation in 1975, and is now the site of the Granary Lane housing development.

Parts of Newport were wired for electricity in the 1920s, much of the work being carried out by Wallace Brothers who had an electrical business on Boat Road, a business which survived until the 1960s. Other Wallace brothers were shoemakers, continuing the tradition started by their father. They had shoe shops, the first one on the site of the present Wormit Post Office and then for many years one in Newport at the bottom of Cupar Road, the upper half of the present Silvery Tay shop.

Wormit however claims to be the first village in Scotland with a domestic electricity supply. This was provided by Alexander Stewart, a

47

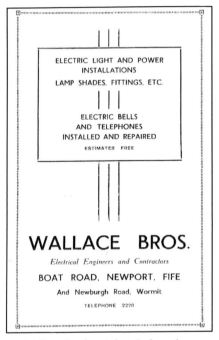

ELECTRIC LIGHT AND POWER
INSTALLATIONS
LAMP SHADES, FITTINGS, ETC.

ELECTRIC BELLS
AND TELEPHONES
INSTALLED AND REPAIRED
ESTIMATES FREE

WALLACE BROS.

Electrical Engineers and Contractors

BOAT ROAD, NEWPORT, FIFE

And Newburgh Road, Wormit

TELEPHONE 229B

Wallace Brothers' electrical services.

Dundee builder. After the opening of the second railway bridge in 1887 Stewart played a major role in Wormit's development in the 1890s. He built Hillpark Terrace and Hill Crescent, as well as many other properties in Naughton Road, Birkhill Avenue and Mount Stewart Road. His Tayside Electric Company offered electricity to all his properties, and probably to others. Sun rays painted on the front of his houses were a symbol showing they were using this new form of power. Possibly the smaller sun symbol found on other houses on Riverside Road and on Netherlea also advertise the use of electricity.

Power was generated by a windmill located on Wormit hill, with a coal-powered steam engine to supplement this when the wind was low. As well as electric lighting for home-owners, basic street lighting was also provided. The generator on the hill was replaced in 1905 by a coal-gas engine down on the main road and this was capable of providing power for cooking as well as lighting. One pricing tariff allowed consumers to pay 10 shillings a quarter and use as much electricity as they liked – how attractive this seems today! This system continued until the 1920s when provision of power was taken over by the Fife Electric Company. After this there were many complaints about the inferior supply!

A Burgh

In 1887 Newport was constituted a police burgh, and its affairs were managed by a provost and a police commission, later the town council. One of the first tasks undertaken by the police commissioners was the proper paving and draining of the streets, which not only benefited travellers on foot or otherwise, but also greatly improved the general appearance of the village.

By the start of the twentieth century the framework of Newport as we know it today was very much in place. As in so many other places across the country, the railway had

Wormit houses with Alexander Stewart's sun symbols.

been the making of Newport and Wormit. Mr James Duncan, first stationmaster at Newport East when the Newport railway opened in 1879, remembered that "for years... trainload after trainload of bricks, stones and building material arrived every week". These building materials were used in the houses that spread in all directions: to the east along Tay Street, Tayview Terrace and Prospect Terrace; up Cupar Road and its arteries to the elegant terraces of Norwood, Linden Avenue and Albert Crescent; through West Newport and up the hill to Kirk Road; and in the creation of an almost entirely new village in Wormit.

Details of Newport's later development in the twentieth century while under control of the town council will be found later in the book in the section Newport the Burgh.

THE CHURCHES IN NEWPORT

The religious needs of Newport have certainly been well catered for, with, until 1978, six active churches in the village, and a seventh, Forgan church, just outside the village itself. In addition, there were two churches in Wormit. To have nine churches here certainly seems disproportionate to the area served by them. How then did the need arise for so many?

The Original Forgan Church

Ruins of old Forgan Church.

Newport was in the old parish of Forgan. The original church of Forgan was first registered (as Forgrund) at St. Andrews in 1150, having been founded in 1124. The church was dedicated to St. Phillan and thereafter the parish sometimes bore that name too. The old Forgan Kirk, now ruined, is situated on the back road to Tayport, and probably dates back to the fourteenth century. Around the kirk is the old

graveyard, in which there are some interesting stones, including those of the Berry family of Tayfield, the Stewarts of St Fort and the Gillespies of Kirkton. The ruined mansion nearby was Kirkton House, home of the Gillespie family. Unusually a modern house has now been built within the ruined walls of the old mansion. Kirkton House was also used as a manse for some time before Forgan manse was built nearby in 1803. Easily seen from the churchyard are the old yew trees in the grounds of Kirkton House: astonishingly these trees have recently been dated as being 1500 years old.

The old kirk was beautifully but inconveniently situated, and it must have been a test of faith indeed for the villagers making their way there from the scattering of cottages on the shore on bleak winter mornings. Small wonder therefore, that, according to the Kirk Session records, the elders were frequently dispatched, mid-service, to scour the Newport braes to round up non-attenders: these reprobates would then in due course be summoned before the Kirk Session to explain their absence. In 1770 the church was thoroughly repaired, then seats installed in the early 1800s. Until the eighteenth century, it was quite rare for churches to be fully seated. Also at the time of these alterations, Newport's boatmen raised money to construct a gallery at the east end of the church. This was known as the Boatmen's Loft. The front face of this gallery was ornately decorated with pictures of Neptune, various nautical instruments and a ferry boat. Despite all these improvements the old kirk's position was still considered too remote. By 1841 the minister, Charles Nairn, was encouraging the building of a new parish church, and this was completed and opened the following year, 1842. The church was to the design of David Bryce, who went on to design Fettes College in Edinburgh. The new church was more conveniently sited, close to the Forgan smiddy, on the Leuchars-Newport road. The old kirk was abandoned, and its contents, and even its windows, roof slates and some stone, were disposed of in 'roup' fashion, and the building rapidly deteriorated. Interestingly, the windows of the old church can still be seen today in the summer-house at Tayfield house. The appropriately named Kirk Road is a present-day reminder of the old path taken by villagers from the Woodhaven end of the village on their way out to both the old and the new Forgan churches. A visit out to the old ruined kirk is much recommended.

The New Forgan Church

New Forgan Church, now a house.

The new Forgan church could seat 600. Early in 1846 it was badly damaged by fire but it was swiftly repaired and continued to be used for almost a century and a half until dwindling membership forced its closure in 1981. It has since been converted to a house.

As Newport grew throughout the nineteenth century, even this new parish church at Forgan could not meet the needs of the rapidly increasing population, and so a new Establishment Church was built in the village at the bottom of Cupar Road in 1870. It was named St. Thomas' as a reminder of the Chapel of St. Thomas of Seamylnes, which in earlier times had stood near the shore.

St Thomas' Church

started. By the autumn work was

St Thomas' Church, now Newport on Tay Church of Scotland.

Planning for the new St Thomas' Church started at a meeting held in September 1866 and a committee was appointed to oversee the raising of the necessary finances. This all-male committee very quickly realised the advisability of also appointing a 'Committee of Ladies'. It's interesting, but perhaps not too surprising, to note that in the first year of fund-raising, 1867, the ladies, as a result of a large bazaar held in the Tayfield grounds and of other activities, were able to raise in excess of £500: the gentlemen meanwhile were only able to raise around £200 through their subscription scheme. During 1868 and 1869 however fund-raising moved on apace, and by the beginning of 1870 work had

complete, and the church was opened on Sunday 6th November 1870.

In these early years St. Thomas' did not have a manse. In October, 1901 therefore, the church embarked on another energetic fund-raising campaign. A Grand Bazaar was held in the Kinnaird Hall in Dundee, in order to raise money to extend the church, install an organ and build a manse. Compared to today's rather modest fund-raising activities this bazaar was on an enormous scale: it lasted four days and raised £2,400, an impressive sum indeed in 1901. With other activities the total sum raised was £4500. With financial objectives achieved, the manse was built the following year next to the church. Substantial alterations were also made to the church. A new chancel and transepts were added at the south end of the building, adding hugely to the church capacity. In addition an organ was installed. Thanks to the perseverance of the organist at that time, W.J. Pae, a magnificent 'Father' Willis organ was installed for the princely sum of £661. Recent refurbishment work on this organ should ensure its lifespan for another hundred years. While all these alterations were being made to the church, members were invited to worship in the Congregational Church.

St Thomas' also lacked hall accommodation. Just across Cupar Road from the church was the Unionist Hall, upstairs from the Cupar Road shops. In the 1920s St Thomas' Church was able to buy this block, acquiring the much needed hall accommodation and also the four shops below which over the years have accommodated a variety of businesses. Most recently two of the shops have been converted into manna coffee shop. The hall became known as Kirk House, and was used until construction of the purpose–built hall behind the manse in 1992. Kirk House was then sold and converted to flats.

Nowadays we take for granted the clock on the church tower, and take for granted its accurate time-keeping. When the church was built funds were raised for the clock in the wider village, not just from potential church members. It was very much seen as a village clock, not just a church clock. The bell for the church clock was donated by Sir John Leng of Kinbrae, actually a member of the Congregational Church, and gas for lighting of the clock was donated by the local gasworks. In the early days there was of course no automatic lighting system: instead the church officer had to climb the tower twice a day to light and extinguish it. For this extra work he was paid just £2 per year.

The Disruption and St Fillan's Free Church

Soon after the opening of the new Forgan Kirk in 1841 came the Disruption of 1843, a controversy which would split the Church of Scotland. Basically the Disruption was a protest by many ministers over the issue of patronage, whereby the local laird held the sole right to appoint a minister to the parish instead of the congregation choosing its own minister. All over Scotland ministers left their churches taking many members with them, to set up Free Churches. Forgan was no exception, and the minister here, Rev. Charles Nairn, and half the members, left Forgan Kirk.

To begin with these dissenters could be found worshipping in a grain loft at Woodhaven Farm, kindly offered by the owner, Mr Rhynd. However

U. F. Church Newport.

St Fillan's Church on William Street, demolished in 1979.

they immediately set about building themselves a new church, and the church which they founded was the Forgan Free Church, later taking the name St. Fillan's Free Church. It stood at the junction of William Street and King Street. The building put up in 1843 was a temporary structure, quickly constructed in just six months with members doing much of the labouring themselves. The house which had been built a few years previously as the Maryton Inn, now Bay House at 12 Tay Street, was used as a temporary manse until the one in Gowrie Street was built. St Fillan's Church was completely rebuilt in 1868. As the church grew and prospered, side galleries were erected in 1890 to accommodate the increased numbers. In 1897 an organ was added, the gift of Mrs Blyth Martin. In 1853 a hall was built next door in William Street which for almost thirty years until 1879 was used as a school. At that time, prior to the Education Act of 1872, the church accepted responsibility for the education of the young, and by opening this school St Fillan's Church was indeed fulfilling this responsibility. The Free Church library was also set up here. This was not just for the benefit of church members, but for everyone in the village, with the annual subscription being just one shilling (5p). Until the Blyth Hall was built in 1877 the Free Church schoolroom was the only place in the village large enough to hold public meetings, and was used very frequently for such purposes.

It's interesting to note that in the 1950s St Fillan's was well ahead in the technology race! Miss Millar of Westwood Terrace had a direct telephone link via the telephone exchange to the pulpit. By the flick of a switch in the pulpit the service could be relayed via the exchange directly to her house. Indeed other members were known to regularly gather there to take advantage of this system. This is clearly the forerunner of today's website sermons. The spire clock at St Fillan's, connected to the master clock in the church below, was a gift from the Misses Millar in memory of their parents.

In 1929 the Established Church of Scotland and the Free Church of Scotland had resolved their differences, to such an extent that the two churches were able to re-unite. In Newport the two churches, St Fillan's and St Thomas', amicably co-existed, sometimes in friendly rivalry, until 1978. Then they united, and the St Fillan's church building was demolished in 1979. The Free Church William Street hall continued to be used by St Thomas' along with Kirk House until their new hall was opened in 1992. The William Street hall, like Kirk House on Cupar Road, was then sold and converted to housing.

In 1981 Forgan Church also joined this union, thus bringing the three congregations together. This union of three churches is now Newport-on-Tay Church of Scotland.

Congregational Church

The only other church in existence in Newport in the early nineteenth century was the Congregational Church, and in fact Newport Congregational Church was one of the oldest Independent congregations in Scotland. It was first formed in 1801, with its first minister appointed in 1803: unfortunately he very soon had to emigrate to escape poverty!

In these early days this congregation met for worship in the ground floor of Broadheugh, the house on West Road owned by the father of the new minister Mr. Thomas Just. Next they met until 1822 in a rented cottage near the pier, which, after being improved and enlarged, became known as the Chapel House. It is highly likely that Dundee missionary Mary Slessor preached here in the Chapel House in the 1870s before her departure to Africa. The Chapel House was only demolished in the 1950s, and is now the site of the Scotscraig retirement homes. The Congregationalists then in 1822 built a small chapel on West Road where they used the upper room, which they occupied until 1868. This building is now 37 West Road, and is a much older building than its present day appearance would suggest.

In 1868 their new church was built at the bottom of Kilnburn. The building also accommodated a hall. Members were always proud to note that theirs was the only church in Newport to have a carillon of bells, presented by member Sir John Leng.

Congregational Church at bottom of Kilnburn, demolished 1991.

This church closed in 1986 and was demolished in 1991. As with most vacant sites in Newport, houses soon filled the gap.

Trinity Church
At the bottom of High Street is Trinity United Free Church, or the United Presbyterian Church as it was earlier. Even before the Disruption of 1843 there had been breakaway groups from the Established Church of Scotland, and three groups of dissenters came together in 1847 as the United Presbyterians. From 1878

Trinity Church at bottom of High Street.

Newport meetings were held in the Blyth Hall, and the first minister, the Rev James Scotland, was appointed in 1879. At that time there was no church, no land for a church and only forty-two members. But in 1881 the foundation stone of this new church was laid by Admiral Maitland-Dougal of Scotscraig Estate, Tayport, and the church opened a year later. The cost of the church was just over £3,000, and every penny was raised by subscription. No fund-raising was carried out. At the opening ceremony a sealed bottle containing copies of the Dundee Courier, Dundee Advertiser, Edinburgh Scotsman and Glasgow Daily Mail, as well as details of the officials of the new church, was laid in the foundations. The architect was C and L Ower, whose name can still be seen carved in the stone wall. Sadly, Trinity Church closed in 2016. The building is on the site of the first Newport Inn erected by the Dundee Guildry in the early 1700s, and from 1840 that building had been occupied by the Post Office. When the site was used for Trinity Church the Post Office found a new home just down the road in the building opposite the pier.

St Mary's Episcopal Church
On the steps above Trinity Church, between High Street and Kilnburn, is St Mary's Episcopal Church. The Episcopalians in Newport set up a congregation in 1883, and their meetings were at first held in the

small Blyth Hall. The first rector, Rev Samuel Hodson, initially met some opposition from local Episcopalians, as at the time they were all attached to St Paul's in Dundee. The advantages of a local church were quickly recognised however, and fund-raising began. Money was speedily raised, with generous contributions being made by the Misses Guthrie of Kilnburnbank, and in particular by Miss Caroline Stewart of St Fort House. In recognition of Miss Stewart's generosity she was asked to lay the foundation stone of the church in 1886, and the church opened the following year 1887. In the cavity beneath the church, the architect, Major Thomas Cappon, deposited a box containing current coins, a list of church office bearers, and copies of the Dundee Advertiser, Evening Telegraph and other newspapers.

The interior of St Mary's must have been fairly austere in its early years, but this is certainly not the case now. Over the years the church has been improved, embellished and beautified, in many cases thanks to the generosity of individual donors. Pulpit, rood screen, font, lectern and beautiful stained glass windows have all been added. Interestingly the organ, which was installed in 1904, was originally water powered before being electrified in 1949. A visit to St Mary's is recommended, and while there, look out for another interesting feature. In some of the

Laying the foundation stone of St Mary's Church in 1886. On the right are the entrance pillars for the Congregational Church, and in the background Newport School.

back pews are carved initials. These are the initials of boys from the Mars training ship. The Captain of the Mars from 1870-1892, Charles Scott, was a member of St Mary's, and some of the Mars boys were marched along here from Woodhaven for Sunday service. Their return to the ship afterwards with the promise of fish stew for lunch can perhaps be seen as bribery!

A final footnote on St Mary's. The church is on the site of an earlier,

St Mary's Episcopal Church on the Kilnburn steps.

and little known, bowling green. This green had been established there by Mr Brown, owner of the Newport Inn, and was in use in the 1850s and 1860s. Further details of this bowling green are in the section Newport at Leisure.

St Fillan's Catholic Church

The flurry of church building in Newport was completed in 1893 with the building of St. Fillan's Catholic Church. In 1886 a Catholic mission had been founded in Newport, and in 1889 the Catholic Church here was raised to the position of a distinct charge. A residence for the priest was purchased in King Street and, until a church could be built, Mass was said in a rented portion of what was the Royal Hotel on the corner of Robert Street and Tay Street. The new church between King St and Queen St was opened in January 1893 by the Bishop of Dunkeld. It would seat around 200 worshippers, and the 1925 Dundee and District

St Fillan's Catholic Church on Queen Street.

Catholic Yearbook remarked on the fact that the church could now accommodate double the number of Mars boys as previously had been able to hear Mass.

The church is of a most unusual construction, being built of corrugated iron and timber. By the end of the nineteenth century, building construction using corrugated iron and timber was becoming very popular, with several companies producing a range of partly prefabricated buildings from which customers could choose a design. Many churches were built using this system, but few remain. St Fillan's is one of the few corrugated iron churches, or 'tin tabernacles' as they were commonly known, that is still used for its intended purpose.

This was the sixth church to be built in Newport in twenty-five years, surely an astonishing record of ecclesiastical building in such a small settlement. Sir John Leng reputedly told a story of being approached on the ferry by a stranger, who said to him, "What a delightful situation; but what a wicked place Newport must be to need so many churches." However as John Leng rightly pointed out, he might also have said, "What saints everyone must be, to have so many sanctuaries."

Wormit Church

Since 1933 Wormit Church has been a united congregation of two former churches, the former West Church on Bay Road, and the former East Church on Riverside Road. The West Church was the Parish Church, and the East Church was the Free Church.

Wormit West Church began in a mission hall in a building converted by the Kirk Session of Forgan for the developing village. Fund raising allowed the construction of a purpose built hall, opened in 1895. The first minister, Rev Robert Mitchell was ordained in 1898. He was the first of five ministers in this church until the union of the two churches in1933. Holding the status of a mission station at first, it became Wormit Parish Church in 1911.

The first Free Church building on the main road site was actually a hall, constructed in 1894-5 for the purpose of Free Church services. It was named the Wormit Free Church Preaching Station. In 1898 the Preaching Station was raised to the status of a Free Church, and the present day church building was

Wormit Church on Riverside Road.

opened in 1901. This church had three ministers until 1933.

After the union in 1929 of the Church of Scotland and the Free Church of Scotland there was no longer a need for two separate churches in Wormit. With the resignation of both ministers in 1932/1933 the union then became possible and desirable. The first minister of the united church was the Rev James Hutchison. Since then the church on Riverside Road has been used, with the Bay Road church being used as hall accommodation and renamed West Hall.

Wormit West Church on Bay Road, now a church hall.

EDUCATION

Forgan School, with the school-house dwarfing the actual school.

One of the earliest schools in the parish was at Wester Friarton, on St Fort land, and shown clearly on the 1855 OS map as St Fort School. This was a small school for the benefit of the children on St Fort estate. Miss Stewart of St Fort supported the school by giving eighteen pounds per annum plus a house and garden to the teacher. The number of children attending was about thirty and the teacher in 1855 was Miss Isabella Bruce.

Until 1843 the main school in the parish was the one at Forgan, known as Forgan Parish School, and now the Forgan Arts Centre. Forgan

Parish School had been established in 1611 but the existing old school building at Forgan opened in 1828, and was extended in 1875. There were generally about 120 pupils in attendance there although these numbers dwindled considerably in the years after World War II. In 1843 when St Fillan's Free Church was built, a school was opened in the hall next door to the church and it became known as Newport Free Church School. Originally intended for the children of Free Church members, it gradually tended to cater for the village children generally, while the Forgan School attracted children from the landward area. Both schools were supervised by their respective

ministers and kirk sessions, and successfully satisfied the educational needs of the parish.

Newport School

Public School, Newport.

Newport School, opened in 1879.

In 1872 the Education Act was passed which legislated for school boards to be established to oversee education in every parish, after which the schools at Forgan and in William Street came under the board's jurisdiction and became known as Forgan and Newport Public Schools. Thanks to the work of the board, a spacious new school was opened in 1879 next to the Blyth Hall. The new school could accommodate 432 pupils and was therefore seen as adequate for the village for the foreseeable future.

This new school replaced the William Street school, and the hall there was used thereafter only for Free Church congregational purposes, and for other village activities. Forgan School continued until 1973, still mainly for country children. When the new school was built in Blyth Street (or Prinlaws Place as it was then known) in 1879, the steps down to the High Street were built to facilitate access from the west.

Until 1949 Newport School provided a full education, covering all

Newport school staff early 1950s.

subjects, until third year in secondary: beyond this stage pupils travelled to Dundee (and Cupar and St Andrews after 1933) to continue their studies. After 1949 the secondary department catered only for those who did not pass the 11-plus examination, taking in such pupils also from Forgan, Wormit and Gauldry schools.

The original building was extended in 1927 when the part of the building towards Scott Street was added. This provided space for more classrooms. From 1960 onwards the school catered for primary pupils only, and was demolished after 1977 when the new primary school was opened on the outskirts of the village, just across the road from the old Forgan School. The opening ceremony of the new school was performed by Dr John Berry of Tayfield. Forgan School had already closed and would find a new lease of life as the Forgan Arts Centre. Within a short time it was being used for various art and craft classes.

Wartime brought changes for pupils, some of these changes being decidedly advantageous, as for much of the Second World War attendance at school was only required in mornings. Excluded from this arrangement however, and no doubt much to their disappointment, were the pupils in the 'qualy' class. This term refers to the qualifying examination, which all pupils sat at the end of primary school. This examination was held in awe by all pupils, and the results determined the type of continuing education that the pupil might follow.

The school had its own air raid shelters. They were at the top of the playground just over the high wall from Scott Street. The bike sheds had to be removed to make room for them. The roofs were of very thick concrete. Jim Smith remembered how quickly they became very stuffy, so much so that the headmaster, John Strath, would stand in the doorway waving a big piece of cardboard to aid ventilation.

Private Schools

There have also been private schools in the village, generally under the supervision of female teachers for girls and young children. For some sixty years or more until 1959, St Fillan's Preparatory School educated hundreds of Newport children. In 1890 this school was established by the Misses Wayman in the house at 33 Cupar Road (the house at the junction of Cupar Road and Hillside Place), and under their leadership young girls were educated up to university entrance. In the early 1930s Miss Davidson took over the school and for the next 23 years Miss Wayman's school became Miss Davidson's school. In the 1940s the school moved to No 18 Kilnburn, and now catered for boys and girls up to age nine. It appears to have been a popular and well respected establishment, with several elderly Newport residents of recent years recalling their happy school days there. After Miss Davidson's retiral in 1953 the school was taken over by Mrs Dunlop until its closure.

Wormit School

There appears initially to have been some reluctance on the part of Forgan School Board to open a school in Wormit: even at the Board meeting of December 1892 it was still being stated that children living there were well within the three miles (stipulated by the 1872 Education Act) of the Board School in Newport. For younger Wormit children there was a very successful and well attended infant school run by Miss Horsburgh. However the rapid expansion of the village following the opening of the new railway bridge and station, combined with a vigorous campaign by Wormit residents, had by 1894 persuaded the School Board to act. Initially it was planned to build the school nearer the station, but eventually land on the south side of the main road was feued from Mr Wedderburn of Birkhill, and work started on a new school on that site. The only remaining evidence today of the school are the iron railings that surrounded it. They still front the houses which were later built on the school site, just to the west of the entrance to Westwater Place.

In the meantime a temporary school was established in the Mission Hall

Wormit School. Opened in 1896.

(above the present shop). The first entry in the school log book was on 3rd September 1894. The teacher Miss Maxwell was introduced and thirty-four pupils were enrolled. By the end of the first week forty-one children were attending. Within a year the number had risen to sixty-five, thus apparently justifying the eventual decision to provide a school in the village.

Wormit Public School opened in January 1896. There was accommodation for 133 children but the building was of a design that could be easily enlarged. Numbers increased rapidly to 140 the following year, and to 165 by 1898. In 1899 an extension of three more classrooms had been added giving accommodation for 200 more pupils. A gym hall and dinner hall were added much later and in World War II an air raid shelter was built in the adjoining playing field.

This school served Wormit until 1978 when it was replaced by the present Wormit Primary School on the site behind the old school, which was later demolished.

Even after Wormit Public School opened, some Wormit families chose to send their daughters to Miss Montgomery's private school. Established around 1900 in the house at 8 Birkhill Avenue, the school later moved to a house on Riverside Road.

The house in Wormit occupied by Miss Montgomery's private school early 1900s.

OTHER BUILDINGS OF INTEREST

Apart from buildings already mentioned, there are various others in the village of some interest, and mostly dating from the 19th century.

Blyth Hall

One of the finest is the Blyth Hall, and Newport is fortunate to have such a splendid public meeting place. The hall was gifted to the inhabitants of Newport by Mrs Isabella Kerr, later Mrs Blyth-Martin of East Newport in memory of her three brothers, Henry, Thomas and Charles Blyth. According to the original deed of gift, the hall was "for the benefit and use of the inhabitants" of the village. The Blyths were a fairly prominent Dundee family. Isabella was married first in 1866 at the age of 48 to William Kerr. William Kerr owned a house on Tay Street (now 72 Tay Street) and gave his name to Kerr Street. When Isabella (Blyth) moved there the house became known as Blyth House. Following his death in 1877 Isabella remarried in 1878, this time to William Martin. The couple took the name Blyth-Martin.

The hall was designed by Mr Johnstone, a Dundee architect, and was opened in 1877. The main hall originally had a gallery at the north end and a tiered stage, and access to the upper small hall was by a staircase at the rear of the stage. In 1890, when accommodation was required for the police commissioners of the recently formed town council, Mrs Blyth-Martin again came forward and provided the money for an extension to the rear to include the municipal offices. A grand inauguration ball was held in the hall in October 1890, attended by all the most prominent members of Newport society at that time. Mrs Blyth-Martin was presented with an illuminated address, (a stunningly beautiful piece of work in book form), and a bust of Mrs Blyth-Martin was unveiled. The bust was the work of Italian sculptor Tadlioni, already renowned for his work at the Vatican, and is still on show in the hall today.

The supervision of the hall was taken over by the town council in 1914, and until the years after World War II the caretaker actually lived on the premises, occupying a flat at the rear of the hall. In 1915 the caretaker's salary was £52 per year, plus free house, lighting and fuel. Between 1973 and 1974 there were extensive alterations and improvements to the hall. The gallery was removed inside the hall, the stage area was altered, a side extension provided better access to the rear and to the upper hall, and new toilets and cloakrooms were

Blyth Hall, Newport

Valentines Series 1343

The Blyth Hall before 1970s alterations. Note tree in street.

added to the front. It was at this time that the false ceiling was added, thus hiding the magnificent ceiling above it. Robert Lorimer, designer of our war memorial and of the National War Memorial in Edinburgh Castle, described this ceiling as one of the finest examples of a pitch pine hammer-beam roof outside the parliament buildings in Edinburgh. In February 1974 a grand Provost's Ball was held to celebrate the reopening of the refurbished hall. This was attended by Provost Randolph Webster and many other local dignitaries. Following local government reorganisation in 1975 the care of the hall was taken over by North-East Fife District Council and is now administered by Fife Council. The most recent development has

been the refurbishment of the library combined with heritage room in 2009.

The flag-pole outside the Blyth Hall was gifted in 1878 by Mr Blyth-Martin. One of the highest in the country it was 120 feet high and extended 20 feet below the ground. It was towed over from Norway and was similar in design to the flag-pole in St. Mark's Square in Venice. The pole, made of pitch pine, was fixed into a large ornamental cast iron base. This casting was made at the Saracen Foundry in Glasgow, the same foundry which produced the Blyth fountain on the Newport braes. In the 1990s the original flag-pole had deteriorated and was replaced with a shorter steel pole. One lesser known use of the flag-pole early in the twentieth century was when the flag was raised to alert local curlers to the fact that ice conditions were good on the curling ponds in Tayfield estate!

Another conspicuous landmark outside the front of the Blyth Hall was a large tree in the street, which, despite the town council suggesting as early as 1919 that it should be removed, was not actually removed until around 1960. James Scrymgeour pointed out that carriages arriving for functions in the hall had to round this obstacle, and that children ran races round it. In 1957 both the tree and the hall frontage were floodlit for Christmas.

The Pier Area

There were several buildings in the area of the pier that are worthy of mention. The ornate pier buildings themselves were erected in 1878 and, along with the buildings opposite, over the years housed many shops: butcher, baker, fishmonger, chemist, stationer, gift shop, painter, police station, post office, grocer and optician. Here certainly was the centre of the village. Stamp vending machines, installed in 1932, are still on the old post office wall opposite the pier. From the 1890s until the 1920s the post office was run by 'Postie Anderson'. A keen amateur photographer, he was responsible for many of the old photographs and postcard views of the village which

still survive today. After the ferry service ended in 1966, Dundee University gradually bought up any of the shops as they were vacated, and established the Tay Estuary Research Centre. Since the university's departure, the pier has been used by a marine services and supplies business. Sadly the other buildings have become increasingly derelict in appearance. Various plans have been lodged with Fife Council for the area's development, but nothing as yet (2015) has been achieved.

Unfortunately gone now are the water wheel and the smiddy. The water wheel was situated in the gully below the High Road, and long ago gave power for grinding meal for the Seamylnes (Seamills). The only visible sign of it now is the large round hole in the old stone wall. This section of wall would have been part of the old mill. The wheel belonged to Tayfield and was gifted to the town council after World War II – instead of preserving it they then dismantled it. The smiddy was just below the wheel, and power from the wheel was used for many of the smiddy tools. The smiddy, also owned by Tayfield, closed in the 1940s, the last tenants being the Don family. Prior to that Willie Young worked the smiddy, and it was his son, John T Young, who established a bicycle repair business on the High Road which developed into the successful Young's garage on Boat

Shops in the beautifully maintained pier buildings.

Road. The garage was demolished in the 1980s to make way for the Scotscraig apartments. Next to the smiddy on the west side, stood the Mission Hall, a fair sized hall eventually demolished in the late 1960s, and the site remains a piece of waste ground. As early as 1927 the council minutes had suggested that the Mission Hall was no longer safe for public use but it outlived that particular death sentence by another forty years! When first erected in the 1820s this building was used as a granary for the new pier. Before the First World War the Mission Hall was used as a Drill Hall for the Newport branch of the 1st Fife Artillery Volunteers. The Volunteers were for some fifty years the precursor of today's Territorial Army, established in 1908. The hall was probably also used by the local Boys' Brigade. When the hall was eventually demolished, local builders bought up the slates from it and from the old granary. It is highly likely therefore that some houses in Newport may still have incorporated in them remnants of these historic buildings.

Further up Boat Road closer to Trinity Church and also accessible from the High Road, was the Chapel House. This has already been mentioned elsewhere in the section on the Congregational Church. Chapel House was demolished in the 1950s and, along with J T Young's garage, would later become the site for the Scotscraig retirement homes.

Balmore, Westwood and Kinbrae

At the east end of what is now West Road, stood the three houses Balmore, Kinbrae and Westwood. All three were magnificent examples of the spacious mansion-houses built in the late nineteenth century for eminent Dundee businessmen. Balmore was built for William Robertson, an iron founder and ex-provost of Dundee, and is the only one of the three still occupied as a private house. Westwood was built for Harry Walker who made his money in jute, and is now St Serf's care home. Kinbrae was unfortunately demolished in 1960 and is now the site of Kinbrae Park

Aerial view showing three mansions.
Top-bottom Westwood, Kinbrae and Balmore. West station bottom right corner.

Kinbrae house, demolished in 1960.

housing estate. It was a magnificent house set in equally magnificent grounds with fountain, stables and glasshouses. Kinbrae was built for Sir John Leng, owner, editor and general manager of the Dundee Advertiser and also founder of the Evening Telegraph and People's Friend. Leng came to Dundee from Hull in 1851. Initially he lived in Dundee then moved to Wellgate House, the white house on the river side of West Road just west of Castle Brae. He didn't have much money when he arrived but by the early 1870s he had amassed enough to build the mansion of Kinbrae. Between 1889 and 1906 he was Liberal MP in Dundee. John Leng was a most enlightened employer, frequently rewarding his employees. This is perhaps best illustrated by the extravagant jubilee fete he hosted at Kinbrae in 1901 to celebrate his fifty years at the helm of the Advertiser. Six hundred guests, employees and their families, crossed to Newport from Dundee on the specially chartered and specially decorated 'Fifie', to enjoy an afternoon at Kinbrae. The visitors were welcomed by Sir John and Lady Leng, they had the run of the extensive gardens, they had a meal with silver service in a marquee, and for entertainment there was the

Mars band, a choir and a conjuror. Sir John Leng is perhaps most widely remembered today for the Leng Medals which are awarded annually to school pupils for solo singing of Scots songs. Also worth a mention is the Leng chapel, built by Sir John as a memorial to his wife Emily. There is further detail on the chapel at the end of this chapter. Eventually Kinbrae came into the hands of the Dunn family, and William Dunn lived there until the 1950s. His son John Dunn was Provost of Newport from 1952 until 1955.

Newport Hotels

The Newport Inn was built by the first Mr John Berry in 1806 to replace the earlier one which had been erected by the Dundee Guildry on the site of the later Trinity Church. The first tenant of the Inn was Mr Gordon of Woodhaven. He was followed by Mr McGregor who died very soon after, but the tenancy was continued by his wife until her retiral in 1840. During this period it was generally referred to in timetables as Mrs McGregor's Inn. The new inn was to begin with a convenient and popular coaching inn, but even after the coaching days were over the inn continued to prosper. For most of the nineteenth century the inn was the place to meet, and according to local news reports, it was regularly used for meetings of the curling club, the

swimming club, the rowing club and the proprietors of the Newport railway to name but a few. Frequent mention is made in the local press of sumptuous meals provided, and lavish entertainment in the beautifully decorated rear hall. In the 1890s it was greatly enlarged by the proprietor Mr Fenwick. There was of course extensive courtyard area and stabling accommodation to the rear of the inn, but this was all demolished by the mid-1960s. In recent years the hotel became rather down-at-heel, but now, in 2015, exciting and imaginative plans for its refurbishment are well under way, and it will no doubt soon return to its former position at the heart of the village's social life.

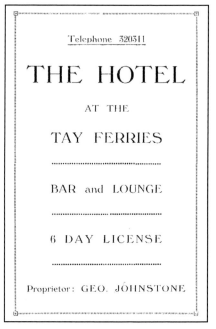

Telephone 320311

THE HOTEL

AT THE

TAY FERRIES

BAR and LOUNGE

6 DAY LICENSE

Proprietor: GEO. JOHNSTONE

Newport Inn.

Other hotels have come and gone. When Mr Dalgleish of Scotscraig founded the village of Maryton in the 1820s, he also established the Maryton Inn. This building is now known as Bay House, at 12 Tay Street. The first four houses in Union Street at the rear of Bay House were the stables for the inn, and no doubt the extensive cellar under the building was an excellent storage area. The only known tenant of the inn was a Mr Thomas Honeyman who would surely do his best to make his business a success. Unfortunately the main route to the ferry pier was not along Tay Street but down Cupar Road. Being situated just too far from the main thoroughfare, the Maryton Inn was doomed to failure. Mr Honeyman fell into arrears with his rent, and was eventually served with a process of eviction. Both the inn and the stables to the rear were converted to houses, possibly around 1840. Bay House was in fact used for some time as a manse for the first minister of St Fillan's Church, which stood further up William Street until being demolished in 1979. The manse for this church was eventually built half-way up Gowrie Street, probably around 1850.

This house on Tay street started life as the Maryton Inn.

Half-way along Tay Street was the Royal Hotel, built in the late 1870s, on the land where the present Royal Buildings block of flats now stands. At first an excellent hotel, its reputation sharply deteriorated until the hotel licence was withdrawn, and the buildings were rented out mainly as dwelling houses, but also as businesses, shops and café. The buildings were also sometimes referred to as Turnbull's Buildings, after the man who built them in 1877. These Royal Buildings were demolished in the 1970s, and in the foundations were found a glass carboy containing newspapers from 1877 and a memorandum written and signed by John Turnbull.

The Seymour hotel, now Riverview Lodge care home on Tay Street, operated as a hotel from 1949 until 1989, but was built in 1898 as a private house. Seymour was built by John Adam St Quentin Leng, son of Sir John. His family lived at Seymour for almost fifty years. Tragically in 1945 one of his sons committed suicide there, and this tragic event probably hastened the sale of the house four years later. It was built at the same time as, and is of very similar design to, Highfield on Kirk Road, now better known as the Leng Home. Highfield was built by Sir John's second son William, and was later re-named Waterstone House. After William's death in 1953 the house was gifted to the council for use as a home for the elderly.

The Royal Buildings on Tay Street which housed the Royal Hotel.

Not far from the Seymour, on the other side of Tay Street, is Craighead House at the bottom of Bank Street. This property also operated briefly as a hotel, probably around 1930. On the small information card issued by the hotel, it can be seen that Craighead House had rather a prestigious telephone number – Newport 1!

Because of the ferry at Woodhaven, there was also an inn there with a farm and brewery on the opposite side of the road connected to it. The brewery produced strong ale and table beer. Like other buildings round about, the inn belonged to the Stewart family of St Fort estate. The inn also offered a horse-hiring service: the horses would be used by the coaches and also by individual travellers. In 1864 the entire innkeeper's effects were sold at a public sale. Mr Grant, the tenant who followed, did not fare much better. He was most distressed when asked to vacate the premises in 1873 in favour of officers from the Mars training ship. This would create great hardship for his family of seven children which included a boy with a recently amputated leg! His beseeching letter and pleas were to no avail, and the building was

This house at Woodhaven was first the Woodhaven Inn, then Mars Cottage.

occupied by the Mars captain and his family until the ship's departure in 1929. It then became known as Mars Cottage.

Other Buildings of Interest

On the bend of Cupar Road, on what was formerly known as "doctor's corner", stands the house which previously held the surgery. In the 1860s the local minister contacted Sir James Simpson (famed for first using chloroform as an anaesthetic) in Edinburgh, and asked him to recommend a young doctor for the village. Doctor John Stewart, a native of Channelkirk in Berwickshire,

duly arrived, and this house Lovaine was built for him. Dr Stewart was later the owner of the first motor car in Newport. The surgery was held in Lovaine Villa for over 100 years. By the late 1890s Doctor John was being helped by his sons Dr Fred and Dr Thomas Stewart. The latter was affectionately referred to as 'Docy Thom', and he eventually took over the practice on his father's death in 1908. Docy Thom also lived at Lovaine. He was assisted by Dr Montague Rust, from all accounts a rather colourful and flamboyant character. Dr Rust practised in Newport for 33 yrs, living first of all

Castle Cottage on West Road, possibly the oldest house in Newport.

at Hollybank on West Road, then at Westcroft, the house at the bottom of Castlebrae which was built for him in 1909. Early in his career he had gone off to help in the Boer War, giving no notice of his departure, but returned safely to continue his work in Newport. He was a great believer in, and practitioner of, spiritualism and faith healing. Much later, he erected a neon sign in his garden at Westcroft to advertise his services. Other doctors clearly didn't think much of this as they reported him, probably to the General Medical Council, for advertising. After the death of his wife in the 1930s he left Newport. He would later return to South Africa, where apparently he sank, and lost, all his money in nursing homes. He died in Cape Town in 1950 aged 76. From the 1930s Lovaine was occupied by Dr Taylor. He was joined in the practice by Dr Mackintosh, who would later be followed by his son and grandson, the present Dr Mackintosh. With six of our doctors from just two families, the father-son tradition has certainly been strong among Newport doctors. From 1965 Lovaine was occupied by Dr McLeod, and the surgery was housed here until a new purpose-built surgery was opened in Victoria Street in 1978. This was extended in 1989 then completely rebuilt and reopened in 2006.

The Yellow Castle. Note the war-time black-out white stripes painted on the kerb stones.

Along West Road there are some fine old houses, many of them dating back to the first half of the nineteenth century. They are thus considerably older than the terraces uphill which date from the arrival of the railway. Probably the oldest is Castle Cottage (1812), sadly uninhabitable for the last thirty years. Despite plans for its restoration, no progress has been made. The cottage had a round room facing the river, and in its early days had specially built curved furniture which was sold with the house. Other houses on West Road are of interest for the varying architectural styles which they illustrate. The

Yellow Castle is certainly the most eye-catching property on West Road. Named for its appearance rather than its function, it dates probably from 1812. It was built by George Just, a stone-mason and member of the Just family who were responsible for building so many of the houses along West Road. The most likely explanation for the Castle's architectural extravagances with its turrets, balconies and varied windows, was that it provided an opportunity for George Just to showcase his building skills. There is no link inside the building between the upper and lower floor, and in the upper part there is an unusual circular hall with balcony. It seems that no members of the Just family ever lived there, and throughout the nineteenth century it was always home to several families at any one time. The Castle was owned by members of the Just family until the 1940s.

At the far end of West Road, before rounding the bend into Wormit, is Netherlea. Netherlea was built in 1891 for Andrew Leitch, director of the Dundee Loch Line Shipping Company. The sun symbols above the roof peaks are probably trademarks of Alexander Stewart, the builder who supplied much of Wormit with electricity (see earlier section on gas and electricity). During World War II the house was occupied by Polish soldiers. From 1948 Netherlea was taken over by the local health board and it became a maternity hospital. After 1974 it became a home for long-stay elderly patients. Despite widespread local opposition Netherlea closed in 2011. Another feature of interest on West Road is the well and horse trough. On the back wall of the trough is the date 1832. The date is of some significance, as it marks the passing of the Great Reform Act, or more correctly the Representation of the People Act of that year. The passing of this Act was the first major attempt to make changes in our system of parliamentary government. The number of men (no women of course) allowed to vote

increased considerably, and other changes were made in the constituencies: for example developing industrial cities were allocated members of parliament for the first time. Although limited in its achievements, the Act was seen as paving the way for further reform, and all over the country the Reform Act was commemorated in the naming of streets and buildings. Here in Newport we have our water trough, and in Dundee the Earl Grey dock was named after the Prime Minister who nursed the Act through parliament. The Hilton Hotel which has recently (2014) been demolished was in fact first named the Earl Grey Hotel because it was built on the site of that dock, and not, as many people believed at the time, named after a popular tea blend! The grassy area immediately behind the trough on West Road was the common bleaching green which could be used by local residents for laundry work, no doubt making use of water from the nearby well.

At the top of Cupar Road on the left hand side before the tennis courts is another fine old mansion. This is Darvel Lodge, built in the 1880s on the site of the former Tayfield Smiddy. The house was built for James Morton who had settled in Newport after coming from Darvel in Ayrshire, the centre of fine lace-making – hence the house's name.

St Fort House.

St. Fort House

St. Fort House, a magnificent mansion house which stood just to the south of Newport and Wormit, was built by Henry Stewart around 1850. The Stewart family owned much of the land on which Wormit and West Newport developed. Robert Stewart, the first member of the Stewart family to live there had bought the estate in 1790. The estate included a house which Robert's nephew Henry demolished to make way for the later mansion, designed by architect William Burn. The family lived in the house until around 1895, after which time it was let to close friends the Pilkington family. They occupied the house until World War II. Miss Maude Pilkington, who grew up there,

would later live in Newport. In 1970, in recognition of all her work for the community, she was one of only two people ever given the freedom of the burgh (see later chapter on the Burgh). According to census returns, the house contained at least 40 rooms spread over two main floors, plus attic rooms in the roof and a basement housing the kitchen and maids' quarters, wine cellar, scullery and stores. During World War II the R.A.F. made use of St Fort house with officers being billeted there, and in the post-war years it was let as a hotel. This venture however enjoyed only limited success, partly due to the local council's reluctance to grant a drinks license. Nor was the building linked to mains electricity, by that time surely a

The magnificent walled garden and glass-houses.

considerable disadvantage in hotel business! In the early 1950s the roof was removed in order to save money on rates. This of course led to the building's rapid deterioration and it was eventually demolished in 1957. The St Fort grounds were extensive and impressive, including woodlands, a curling pond and walled garden with greenhouses supplying the house with flowers, fruit and vegetables. The present main road more or less follows the line of the old drive up to the house from the five roads roundabout. This new main road, which was built in the 1960s at the time of the Tay Road

Bridge construction, cuts the St Fort Estate in half. The old walled garden can still be seen to the east of the main road. Nearer the house were the home farm, stables, a laundry, a doocot, an icehouse and a creamery. The creamery was a most unusual little building with thatched roof supported by wooden props. The verandah was beautifully tiled and the windows were of leaded glass. The creamery supplied milk, butter and cream to the family in St Fort House and to all the other families on the estate. It was probably in use as a dairy until the 1940s and has recently been restored. The doocot

Curling at St Fort.

The impressive coat of arms above the front door is preserved today in one of the houses on the estate.

The estate dairy, still easily recognised today.

has also been restored. Just to the north of where the house stood, it dates from 1733. The parkland in front of the house was known as the 'greens', and was frequently the setting for the meeting of the local hunt, and in more recent years for carriage-driving championships. The farm and parkland look very much the same today as they did in 1850, and many of the trees planted by the early Stewarts can still be identified. Although over the years there has been further significant planting, much of the landscape of St Fort is still recognisable from original drawings laid out by William Burn. Sadly only the house is missing.

Leng Memorial Chapel

Leng Memorial Chapel

The chapel is on a hilltop, two miles south of Newport, and is most evident when floodlit at night. It was built by Sir John Leng between 1895 and 1897 as a memorial to his first wife Emily, who was the first person to be interred in the surrounding Vicarsford cemetery. Prior to that, burials had been at the old Forgan Kirk. Designed by architect Thomas Cappon, the chapel is in the thirteenth century Gothic style and modelled on Sainte Chapelle in Paris. The vaulted interior is faced with creamy Normandy stone. On one wall is an inscription about Lady Leng and on another wall is a memorial to the five Newport men who gave their lives in the Boer War. The chapel is very often open on the local Doors Open day, and a visit is recommended.

THE BERRY FAMILY AND TAYFIELD

Tayfield House

Throughout the previous pages there has been frequent mention of the Berry family and Tayfield Estate. Indeed many aspects of the village development have been dependent on the co-operation of Tayfield. The village has been fortunate to have developed alongside an estate and a family which have always held the interests of the village very much at heart.

The first John Berry (1725-1817) bought the land of Inverdovat in 1788 and built his house, so forming the estate of Tayfield. The land bought by John Berry probably covered most of Newport as we know it today, and also part of the land of the present Inverdovat Farm. His wife was in fact a descendant of the Nairne family of Sandford (the early name of Sandford later changed to St. Fort). The "de Narnes, Narnes and latterly Nairnes of Sandford" had owned land in this area since at least the 14th century. By building his house at Tayfield John Berry was in fact setting up home on land which had long been owned by Mrs. Berry's forebears.

John Berry died in 1817, and the task of further developing the estate would be continued by his son William. One major achievement of the family was the building of the turnpike road to Newport in 1808. Only after building a mile of the road themselves on their own land did they manage to persuade the turnpike trustees that a road should be continued to the Newport pier. The benefits of this road to the village have already been described.

William Berry (1774-1852), a Writer to the Signet in Edinburgh, was in a fortunate position financially, and was able to develop and extend the estate. In addition to the land bought by his father, William Berry added to the estate in 1834 by acquiring the farm buildings and land of Causewayhead from the Scotscraig Estate and, possibly at this time too, the farms of Waterston Crook, Strawberrybank and Craighead.

Since these early days the extent of the estate has altered, and several factors have contributed to this. Fairly large areas of land have been feued or gifted to the village, and the land has been used in the main for housing, new roads or for recreational purposes.

Throughout the nineteenth century, plots of land in both East and West Newport were feued, not just for house-building but for other purposes also, such as the building of churches and the Blyth Hall. In the twentieth century too, land has been used for house-building, in many cases being sold to the town council for local authority housing. The largest area of land was lost in the 1960s when fifty acres were acquired by the road bridge authorities for the road bridge approach roads.

Other areas have been gifted to the burgh, mainly for leisure use. According to the burgh minutes, it was as early as 1897, for the grand amount of £1 per annum, that the town council accepted management and control of the Braes, but with ownership being retained by Tayfield Estate. Gowrie Woods were also soon leased from Tayfield, and in 1946 the woods were given to the council by Dr. John Berry (1907-2002), father of the present owner William. Gowrie Wood was gifted for recreational purposes but he also suggested it might possibly be a bird sanctuary. As an expert in all things to do with nature conservation, this would clearly be a suggestion close to his heart. A condition of the gift was that there should be no building on the land. He also gave to the burgh the Gas Lane area (later Granary Lane) and the old pier. The land containing the water wheel and the Mission Hall had been transferred to the council earlier by Dr Berry.

At the present time however the size of the estate is still considerable. Apart from Tayfield House itself and the grounds around it, the estate covers Northfield, Inverdovat, Causewayhead and Easter Friarton farms, and Seamills Cottage. Victoria and Kinbrae Parks, also still parts of the estate, are leased to Fife Council.

Tayfield Grounds

Credit must be given to the first John Berry and the first William Berry for the planning and most of the landscaping of the grounds around Tayfield House. They carried out extensive tree planting on landscape design principles. A beech tree that fell in a gale of 1973 was found to be about 180 years old. This ties in precisely with the date of that early planting done by John Berry. A bill was found in the house for fifty trees purchased at that time: possibly the beech tree was one of them. More recently, in 2012, the Tree Register of the British Isles measured several of the trees in Tayfield. Some were recorded as being the biggest in Fife. The beech tree behind the Duck Pond was, at 39 metres, the tallest beech in Scotland as recorded by the Tree Register. It is difficult to imagine that when Tayfield Estate was first established there were very few trees there at all. This tree-planting programme is very much a continual process with trees constantly being replaced, and since John Berry's day, it has been continued by succeeding generations until the present day. The family has a tradition of marking births and special family occasions by planting trees, and this is continued today. The beauty of the grounds around Tayfield bears witness to all these efforts, and, thanks to the family's generosity in allowing fairly free access, the grounds can be appreciated and enjoyed by all.

Tayfield foresters

The bee house

Under William's guidance the north and south drives were laid out and the lodges built: the north lodge at the High Road entrance dates from 1821 and the south lodge on Cupar Road from 1830. The north lodge was to the design of architect James Gillespie Graham, known for projects such as Moray Place in Edinburgh, and more locally for Cupar County Buildings and Crawford Priory near Cupar. The south lodge was possibly designed by George Smith, the architect responsible for the 1830 alterations to Tayfield house (see Tayfield House below). Abercraig, the first house on the north of West Road, was built in 1840 as the dower house for the Berry family. A dower house

was owned by an estate and was usually occupied by the widow of the estate owner, hence the title 'dowager'. The widow would move into the dower house thus vacating the family house for the son and heir. The Tayfield dower house was never used in this way but instead was occupied in the mid-1800s by Margaret and Sarah Berry, two sisters of the first William Berry. The house was eventually sold in 1989.

Immediately in front of the house are the grass tennis courts. These were laid out by estate overseer William McLaren towards the end of the 19th century. According to Jim Smith the turf was brought down from Inverdovat, and the courts were particularly weed- and moss-free. The estate staff were encouraged to play on the courts to keep the turf firm.

Close to the house to the north-west was the ice-house. Prior to the invention of the refrigerator, such structures were used to store ice throughout the year. Like many others, the Tayfield ice-house was basically an underground chamber with a stepped entrance. In winter ice would be collected from the nearby mill ponds and packed into the ice-house where it would remain frozen for many months. Sometimes extra insulation was provided by packing the ice with straw or sawdust. The ice could then be used throughout the year for preserving food, for cooling drinks or for preparing elaborate iced

Summer house

desserts. When the ice-house was no longer needed for its original purpose it served as a very convenient coal store!

To the south-west of the main house lie the buildings of the home farm. These incorporated a house and bothy for estate workers. The buildings on the south side of the courtyard were later converted to the Garden House, looking out over the walled garden. The walled garden is an acre in extent. Jim Smith recalled the immaculately trimmed and symmetrically laid out grass paths, eight feet wide herbaceous borders, fruit trees and vegetables. At the centre of the garden was a sundial, now repositioned. There was also a whale jaw bone over the east entrance to the garden until it eventually collapsed.

Between the home farm and the Mill Dam Pond is a fresh water spring. This water was said to have a high magnesium content and as such would have certain health benefits. For this reason, according to Berry family lore, in the nineteenth century the water was sold in Dundee for one penny per bottle. During World War II the spring water was tested to check its purity. Being pronounced of good quality, it could have been used as an alternative emergency water supply for the village if the need arose.

Outside the rear wall of the walled garden is a most unusual and

Den cottages

colourful structure. This is a Victorian bee house, one of only five known in Scotland, and probably the only wooden one. It has now been listed as a building of historical importance. It is believed to have been brought to Tayfield by boat around 1850. The actual hives were on shelves inside, with a different coloured entrance for each hive. Did the bees recognise the colours, or did they home in instinctively on their own hive? The hives could be worked from inside the bee house, and each hive had a glass observation window on its rear wall. It was probably last used in the 1950s.

To the west of the house is what in earlier times must have been a rather grand summer-house. This dates at least from the 1840s, possibly many years earlier, and is an excellent example of early recycling! When the new Forgan church was opened in 1841 parts of the old kirk building on the back road to Tayport were removed. Some of the windows were put to good use as part of the Tayfield summer-house. In front of the summer-house was a circular rose garden. It's interesting to see from the postcard view on the previous page, that at sometime the summer-house was used as a poultry house.

To the rear of the summer-house is the former dairy. William Berry recently commissioned the restoration of the dairy, and recalls

The Duck Pond, complete with fountain.

the years when this little building was used by his great aunt to make cream and butter from the milk of the house cow.

In the extreme west of the Tayfield grounds, on the edge of the wooded area towards Kirk Road, are the ruins of the Den cottages. These cottages were in the most idyllic setting, and were the subject of many picture postcards. They are still fondly remembered by those who lived there, and were particularly noted for the attractive and productive gardens. At the start of the last century, they were used by the then Mrs Berry for charitable purposes, as they were offered as holiday homes for workers and invalids from Dundee, and as a place of rest and relaxation for London city missionaries. But more recently, with no mains water or power supply, life there must have been difficult, and the cottages were closed by the town council in the 1950s. Sadly they were subsequently set on fire accidentally and burned down.

One of the pleasures of a walk in the Tayfield grounds is the variety of birds to be seen, especially around the ponds. The original Upper and Lower Mill Dam Ponds were dammed to provide power via a wooden water wheel for the original Seamills and later for the smiddy machinery. The Duck Pond south of Tayfield House was excavated by spade and barrow at the end of the mechanical digger, to provide additional islands as nesting sites. Over to the west of the grounds are the old Curling Ponds, one still with water in it. These were used by the local Curling Club (see section Newport at Leisure).

Tayfield grounds were not always quite as freely accessible as they are today. From at least the middle of the nineteenth century and into the twentieth, permission to walk in the grounds had to be obtained and permits were issued.

Tayfield House and Family

View of house from south.

Tayfield House was built in 1790, and the architect is thought to have been Robert Anderson. In 1830 extensive additions were made to Tayfield House, to the design of architect George Smith. Smith had recently completed his Exchange coffee house in Dundee, the building which would later house the Assembly Rooms and later David Winter's printing business. At Tayfield the roof was altered, a new section was built on the west side and a completely new south front was added. These alterations almost doubled the accommodation in the house.

92

Domestic staff around 1900.

Until World War II a large staff would help to run the house. In 1911 for example there were eight live-in servants, plus outdoor workers such as groundsmen, gardeners, foresters and grooms who lived elsewhere on the estate, and daily staff from the village also. Very often there was a French or German speaking Swiss governess, or table-maid who only spoke her own language while at work: this would encourage the family's language skills.

Following World War II there were numerous outbreaks of dry and wet rot in the house which were contained but not always fully restored. After the death of William Berry in 1954 and his sister 'Miss Annie' in 1956, Dr and Mrs John Berry created a flat for themselves on the second floor of the house.

From 1963 until 1988 rooms on the ground and first floors were used as accommodation for a nursery school for the children of the village. The children could enjoy and appreciate the beautiful surroundings.

When Dr and Mrs John Berry moved to the Garden House in 1989, William and Elizabeth Berry undertook a major restoration of the house before moving into it themselves in 1991 – exactly 200 years after the first John Berry moved into the new house he had built.

Over more than two centuries the link between the Berry family and the village has been close. However there is no doubt that as time has passed the nature of that relationship has changed. The feuing of land for building in the village in the nineteenth century may have given the feuars the right to build their properties, but at the same time the estate retained a close interest in the land and could impose certain conditions on what might be built where. At a time when no other planning regulations were in existence, this ensured some measure of control over the village's development. Newport therefore escaped some of the less attractive and haphazard expansion seen elsewhere, and we still benefit from that today. In earlier times Tayfield also provided numerous employment opportunities within the village, both in the house and on the estate. As an indication of the close relationship between the Berry family and the village, it's interesting to note the enormous enthusiasm shown in the village in 1858 when the second John Berry (1824-1877) married Margaret Burn-Murdoch in Edinburgh. In celebration Newport was decorated on the wedding day with flags and bunting. Streamers flew from houses and chimney pots and a bonfire was lit in the evening. Free ale was given out to all. In the evening all the tenants on the estate, and other local gentlemen, had a sumptuous meal in the Newport Inn.

The Berry family has now lived at Tayfield for well over 200 years, and still show a keen interest in the affairs of the village. The names John and William are given to the eldest sons in the family in alternate generations, and at Tayfield now we have in William Berry the sixth generation of the family since the first John Berry in 1788, with the seventh and eighth generations frequent visitors.

The Berry Family of Tayfield

John Berry 1725-1817   m. (1) Janet Fraser (2) Isabella Law
                                    1 son, 5 daughters

William Berry 1774-1852   m. Isabella Henderson
                                    2 sons, 4 daughters

John Berry 1824-1877   m. Margaret Burn-Murdoch
                                    4 sons, 2 daughters

William Berry 1864-1954   m. Wilhelmina Barns-Graham
                                    1 son

John Berry 1907-2002   m. Bride Fremantle
                                    2 sons, 1 daughter

William Berry 1939-   m. Elizabeth Warner
                                    2 sons

John 1976-   m. Megan Bastick
                                    2 sons

William 2008-

THE MARS TRAINING SHIP

No study of Newport's past would be complete without some mention of the Mars training ship, which was for so many years a familiar sight moored out in the river off Woodhaven pier. The Industrial Schools Act (1866) had led to the establishment of a number of training ships around the shores of the United Kingdom and one of these was the Tay training ship. The Mars had enjoyed a fairly short and uneventful spell of active service before being anchored in the Tay to serve as a training ship for the east of Scotland. From 1869 until 1929 the ship enjoyed a close relationship with Newport, with the Mars boys taking part in many aspects of village life.

News of the ship's imminent arrival caused great excitement up and down the coast, and Captain Scott later wrote in 1917 that "every boy with sea-faring instincts wanted to get to the Mars". On 17th August 1869, enormous crowds turned out to view her arrival: at two hundred feet long and sixty feet wide she was easily the largest ship to have entered the estuary. In fact the sight of this great warrior being tamely towed up the river combined with her shabby unpainted appearance must have caused considerable disappointment to some onlookers. At first the ship was moored far out

towards the middle of the river, making it very vulnerable to the storms that swept down the Tay. From 1875 it was moved closer to the Fife shore with new moorings just 300 yards from Woodhaven pier. This clearly was much safer for both boys and ship.

The Boys
The Mars provided a naval-type training for up to 400 young teenage boys. Despite its bad boy reputation, none of these boys, with possibly the odd exception, had ever been convicted of any crime, their only wrong-doing perhaps being truanting from school. The majority were what we would now call 'at-risk' boys: they were from poor backgrounds, from broken homes, were orphaned, homeless or destitute, and were hopefully being rescued from the life of crime which they might otherwise enter. The boys were sent to the Mars between the ages of 12 and 14 (in later years age 11), and did not stay beyond the age of 16.

There is a general belief and acceptance in the Tayside area that the majority of the boys on the Mars were from this area. Statistics however do not bear this out. For example in 1890 of the 398 boys aboard only 83 were from Dundee, with by far the largest number being from Glasgow. A similar pattern can

Life on board Mars must have seemed a million miles away for these local lads skinny-dipping off the end of Woodhaven pier.

be seen in other years. Some came from much further afield. James Martin, a London lad, came to the Mars in the 1920s and indeed was one of the last boys on board. As an adult, he resettled in London, but continued to visit Newport for as long as he was able. I was fortunate to meet him on several of these visits in the early 1990s. His arrival on the Mars had been traumatic to say the least. When very young, his parents had separated and his mother found great difficulty caring for James and his sister. She found a post in London as a housekeeper, but she was only allowed to have her daughter with her, and she had to find another home for eleven-year-old James. She

heard of the Mars, and duly put him on the train for Dundee, asking a lady in the carriage to keep an eye on him! The terrors of that journey for a small lonely boy cannot be imagined. Perhaps the most alarming moment for him would come as his train crossed the great Tay estuary and he had his first sight of the ship that would be his home for the next four years. He was duly met at Dundee station by an officer from the Mars, and taken by ferry to Newport. They then walked to Woodhaven where James had his head shaved, was issued with uniform clothing and given a number. He would be known by that number for the next four years.

The Staff

During the sixty years that the Mars was on the Tay, there were just four superintendents in command of the ship. The first to take charge, and only very briefly as he was dismissed in less than a year, was Captain Baldwin Wake. He was followed by the very able and popular Captain Charles Scott who captained the ship until his death in 1892. His son Captain Augustine Scott followed until his retiral in 1919. For almost fifty years the ship had been supervised by father and son, both men being fully devoted to the task and earning much admiration for their work. For the final ten years until its departure in 1929 the ship was under the command of Captain Henry Heathcote.

The captains were assisted on board by other skilled staff members: schoolmasters, technical instructors and bandmasters all played their part in imparting knowledge and maintaining discipline among their young charges. Many members of staff were exceptionally loyal, serving for long periods. Mr Thomas was senior school master for twenty-two years, Messrs Barlow and Flynn served as officers for seventeen and twenty-five years respectively, Mr Gillespie was an instructor for eighteen years and Mr Stovin was assistant teacher for 20 years before going on to be superintendant of the Cardiff shipping home. Because so

many of the Mars boys who joined the Navy shipped from Cardiff, a house was acquired there in 1895 to accommodate them while awaiting their ships. There is no doubt however that the most extraordinary period of service was by ship's carpenter Alexander McDougall. He was the first officer to join the Mars on the day in 1869 that the ship anchored in the Tay. He gave fifty years of loyal service and in 1919 a ceremony of thanks was held on board to mark his retiral at the age of 79. During the first nineteen years he had no holidays. A different form of loyalty was shown by William Bowman. Orphaned by the death of his father in 1900, he came to the Mars aged 11. He stayed for four years, but returned in 1910 to become a technical instructor under the leadership of technical master Richard Burns.

Inevitably there were also staffing problems. According to school-master Mr Thomas there would always be difficulties recruiting teachers due to poor pay, lack of privacy and the conditions aboard. In the early years there was a fairly regular turnover of staff despite attempts to prevent this by raising salaries and improving living conditions for the masters. In the early 1870s schoolmaster salaries were fixed at £50 per annum, but by 1905 the head schoolteacher Mr McBeth was being paid £140. Bandmasters were paid much less than the schoolmasters so many of them did not last long in the job.

Close confinement on board caused problems among staff as well as the boys. Members of staff were expected to conform to strict behavioural standards and sometimes this proved too difficult, especially for those not used to naval standards of discipline. Some members of staff were dismissed for disobeying orders, and on one occasion some cooks were dismissed for embezzling ship stores. There were the inevitable accusations of mistreatment of the boys against members of staff, and sometimes staff members were dismissed as a result. Conversely however, the lifestyle on board also allowed opportunities for bravery, and more than one member of staff was recognised for saving life.

Training and Discipline

The naval training, under the supervision and leadership of the ship's captains, former captains of the Royal Navy, provided a good grounding in seamanship, and indeed many of the boys went on to follow a naval career, some in the Royal Navy but many more in the Merchant Navy. The reason for this difference in numbers is that many of the Mars boys quite simply did not meet the physical requirements at that time of the Royal Navy: the standard height requirement was 5 feet 1 inch and the required chest measurement was 30 inches. Such failings no doubt reflect the standard of living of these boys in early life.

The boys were strongly disciplined, especially in the earlier years, and the discipline was helped by the use of the 'tawse', the leather belt widely used in all Scottish schools. Most feared however was an encounter with the 'black cuddy', the punishment for any serious misdemeanours. This involved being laid face down over the vaulting horse and being tied by wrists and ankles, before 6-12 strokes of the belt were publicly administered. For many of the boys, including Jim Martin, only one experience of this painful and humiliating practice was enough. While on board the boys were always known by their number and not by their name. On the whole however the discipline was very fair, and the atmosphere on board was generally a happy one. As Linda McGill accurately points out in her book The Mars Training Ship (1996), life ashore for these boys at that time would not have been any better. In photographs from later years longer hair is to be seen: perhaps an indication of some relaxing of discipline. Certainly when William Bowman returned to the ship as an instructor he believed the boys were much better treated by then.

Other skills were also developed

Boat drill for the boys at Woodhaven.

and the boys were given training in woodwork, metalwork, shoe-making, tailoring and gardening. In the early years of the twentieth century it was becoming apparent that in the new century there would be less need of skills in seamanship, but more need of practical skills. Workshops were set up on shore at Woodhaven, where the boys were able to develop these practical skills. These workshops were built and fitted out by Richard Burns assisted by some of the boys, and were completed in 1908. Many items made by them were sold locally, and there are still numerous tea trays, chess boards and other items made

by the boys still in existence. Kitchen gardens were laid out too: hence the present-day street name Mars Gardens. The vegetables produced were used on board ship, and the surplus sold.

Daily Routine

Days on Mars followed a regular routine, with the boys working hard, observing strict discipline and enjoying little if any privacy of any sort. The early morning bugle call at 5 am in the summer and 6 am in winter was followed by a prayer and a cold water wash. Next came the hated deck-scrub before breakfast at 7.30. After breakfast the boys

Showing off their achievements outside the Mars workshops on Woodhaven pier.
Many such items still exist locally today. Photo courtesy of Fife Cultural Trust.

gathered for inspection, and for any punishments to be publicly administered. Then it was into the classroom or workshops until lunchtime. These classes continued in the afternoons until teatime at 5 pm. The only real leisure time enjoyed by the boys came in the early evening when they could participate in various supervised leisure activities. Bed was at 8.45 pm. Sundays offered a welcome break from routine with, notably, no deck-scrub! After Captain's inspection the boys headed off to church services, many of them marching into Newport for services at St Mary's Episcopal Church on the steps above the High Street, and considerable numbers attending the Catholic St Fillan's Church in King Street. A Church of Scotland service was held on board. With no classes on Sundays the boys had more opportunity for sport and leisure activities, both on board and ashore. Inevitably some boys attempted to escape the harsh environment, some with tragic consequences. Perhaps the most notable were the three young lads who in 1871 were lost as they tried to make their escape by a sailing boat. Their 'waywardness' is recalled on their gravestone in the

Not the most comfortable of bedding arrangements.

old Forgan kirkyard. Others attempted to relieve the boredom and monotony by engaging in boyish pranks: this despite the sure knowledge of the stern punishments that would follow. Of much more concern however were several incidents of fire-raising, a serious worry on board a wooden ship some distance from shore. The water pipe which was brought to the ship from Woodhaven after 1881 perhaps helped to allay this fear of fire. Following one outbreak of fire a telephone line was installed to enable speedy summons of help. Outbreaks of disease were also inevitable in such a close-knit community. Thanks to the generosity of Mrs Stewart of St Fort, the granary building at Woodhaven pier was put to good use, and converted to serve from the 1880s onwards as a 30-bed hospital for the boys from the Mars. Until the hospital was available it had been extremely difficult if not impossible to contain outbreaks of serious disease on board. In the early years the ship had to be evacuated to allow thorough fumigation: evacuation of four hundred boys was no easy task. Even after the availability of the hospital facilities emergencies occurred, with boys being sent ashore to escape infection from scarlet fever, typhoid and other diseases.

Leisure Time

A fine gymnasium was fitted up on board ship and a swimming bath constructed at Woodhaven pier. Before this was built, a wrecked ship was moored astern of the Mars and was fitted out as a floating swimming bath. In 1871 a schooner Lightning was purchased and was used on the North Sea to give the boys sea-going experience. It was replaced in 1881 by the brig Francis Molison, donated by the widow of the Executive Committee's first President. Each year the Francis Molison made a trip around the coast of Britain, and the change of routine which this voyage provided was much looked forward to, as was, for the same reason, the annual summer camp at Elie. From 1899 onwards the boys had a five-week visit to Elie, where they were billeted in a disused granary beside the harbour. Although later on the boys travelled to Elie by train, at first they walked there, camping en route, and Jim Martin remembered eating raw vegetables stolen from fields on the way.

It seems that any opportunity of finding extra food was eagerly followed up by the Mars boys. As growing lads they had healthy appetites which were not always satisfied by the fairly meagre and monotonous rations on board. Any chance of an onshore excursion, for whatever reason, provided the opportunity of more food! Musical talent presented that chance for many of them. The ship had a competent brass band which was regularly invited to perform at many functions both locally and further afield. Any performance was usually followed by a splendid tea party for the boys. Members of the pipe band and the choir also enjoyed this privilege, and provided an added incentive to play or sing to the best of their ability. Occasionally some of the boys were invited to be beaters at game shoots on local estates: again these positions were much sought after as they would share in the hearty picnics provided.

On the whole the boys were very well thought of in the immediate neighbourhood. Because of their good behaviour on shore there were many requests for performances by bands and choir, and also for gymnastic displays. Such onshore excursions were hugely enjoyed by the boys as they also provided a much appreciated change of routine. It's pleasing to know that for many years the Newport Club sent their huge supply of the previous month's magazines to the Mars. These would no doubt prove of great interest to all. Over the years the Mars had several patrons who provided occasional treats for the boys. These treats might take the form of an outing somewhere, the provision of small Christmas gifts, or some entertainment or other. Needless to say these treats, in whatever form, were much enjoyed by the boys.

DUTY'S CALL.   H.M.S. *Francis Molison*   3. A. M. A. Series.

More nautical training for the boys, this time on the Francis Molison.

The Mars and World War I.

The outbreak of war in 1914 would affect all Mars boys, both past and present. By 1915, an estimated 400 ex-Mars boys were already serving in the armed forces, and many more would follow. Some found themselves in various branches of the army, battling over No Man's Land on the Western Front, or perhaps playing a small part in the Gallipoli campaign, but for many, the naval skills learned on board the Mars naturally led them into the navy. Many would pay the ultimate sacrifice: in total 170 Mars boys died for their country. Their memorial, unveiled in 1921, stands at Woodhaven harbour.

For the boys on board, the threat of war was close. The Mars might well be a target for naval attack, and it was decided that for their safety, they would sleep onshore in their workshops at Woodhaven. Meanwhile they too could contribute to the war effort. They doubled their horticultural efforts, and their vegetable gardens at Woodhaven were made even more productive. In this way they contributed to the national food supply, supporting the government initiative to produce more home-grown food, at a time when it was essential to cut back on supplies coming from abroad.

In November 1918 the end of the war was celebrated locally, and as part of these celebrations on Armistice Day there was great activity among the ships on the Tay.

The Mars pipe band.

Just after ten in the morning on 11th November ships picked up the news of the Armistice over their wireless and immediately used their sirens to proclaim the news. A bunting-bedecked Mars proudly joined in with the warships, destroyers and minesweepers.

The End

By the 1920s it was gradually being accepted that the type of training provided by the Mars was no longer needed, and that inevitably the ship's days were numbered. This view however was not universally held. The minutes of a Newport Town council meeting in 1922 for example, refer to the possible removal of the ship, and quite clearly state the councillors' wish for it to be retained. In 60 years the Mars had taken over 6500 vulnerable, at-risk boys off the streets and provided security, discipline and skills for their future. In 1919 at the ship's jubilee celebrations, it had been pointed out that monitoring of ex-Mars boys showed that 95% of them went on to follow decent lives. This in itself was a quite remarkable achievement.

But throughout the 1920s the number of boys on board was reducing, and concerns were increasing about the condition of the ship itself. In May 1929, on grounds of safety, the remaining boys were transferred ashore to occupy the workshops. On the morning of 27th June 1929 the Mars was towed down-river, watched from

Woodhaven by the last boys and staff, and given a final salute from the horns of many of the ships in Dundee harbour. Her final destination would be the ship-breaking yard at Inverkeithing.

In August all the remaining items of equipment from the Mars, from the schoolroom, kitchen, gym and workshops, was auctioned off at Woodhaven pier. The workshops themselves, where so many Mars boys had learned the skills which would stand them in good stead in future life, found a new lease of life.

They were taken over and put to good use for many years by the local Scouts.

*Mars boys watch from Woodhaven as the ship starts on its journey
to the breaker's yard at Inverkeithing.
(C) John Cameron, with the permission of his granddaughter.*

NEWPORT THE BURGH

The coat of arms, granted in 1956.

As has already been mentioned, Newport acquired in 1887 the status of a police burgh. Initially the burgh covered only the area of East and West Newport but in 1902 the boundaries were extended to include Woodhaven and Wormit. At Wormit Bay, set flat in the grass close to the memorial for the victims of the Tay Bridge disaster, is the boundary stone. 'NPB' on the stone indicates the limits of Newport Police Burgh. The burgh was divided into three wards, Ward 1 being Newport east of Cupar Road, Ward 2 west of Cupar Road and Ward 3 Woodhaven and Wormit.

For almost 100 years until local government reorganisation in 1975, the affairs of the burgh were managed first of all briefly by the police commissioners and then by the elected town council. The council consisted of Provost, Senior and Junior Bailies and six other councillors. All manner of problems had to be faced and dealt with, and the smooth running of the village affairs throughout that period owed much to the dedication of these councillors.

The first provost of Newport was Provost Alexander Scott of Ashbank Villa on Tay Street. He served as provost for three terms of office and in recognition of this period of service Scott Street was named in his honour and a silver rosebowl and salver were presented to him by the community. These items would be the start of an impressive collection of burgh regalia. This collection would also eventually include the burgh halberd, chains of office for the provost and for the two bailies, the Windmill Park gold key and an inkstand presented to the council in 1951 by William Berry – this had been donated to him by the defunct quoiting club. Perhaps the most stunning item in the burgh collection was the illuminated scroll presented to Mrs Blyth Martin in 1890 to acknowledge her generosity in extending the hall to the rear. Many of these items are now on display in the library heritage area.

There were 28 provosts between 1887 and 1975, most of them serving for a period of three years. To introduce a note of humour, it's interesting to note that Provost George Rain Little in the 1930s was followed by Provost Frank Fairweather! Where else but in Newport, on the east coast of Scotland with its low rainfall, would we find this? There are photographs of all 28 provosts in the foyer of the Blyth Hall.

In 1956 the burgh was granted a coat of arms. The motto of the burgh was Dei Flumen Nobis Lumen meaning The River of God is our Saving Light. The blue and silver lines at the base of the shield and the galley above symbolised the river and the ferries. The ship bears on its sail the arms of Nairne of Sandford (St Fort) while the lion with the cross in the stern comes from the arms of Berry of Tayfield: most of the burgh was built on the lands of these estates.

Ornate lamp posts were erected outside the home of the serving Provost. When in office there were two lamps at his gate, and when he retired one was removed. The glass lanterns were beautifully patterned and bore the Provost's initials and the years of his term of office. The lantern was surmounted by a crown. Few of these remain in the village today. However a complete lamp standard still stands outside the house of Provost Randolph Webster (1971-1974) in Woodmuir Crescent,

The ornate lamp standard outside the house of provost Randolph Webster.

and the lamp posts and lanterns minus the glass can still be seen at the entrance to the Parish Church. The last Provost of the burgh, the Rev. Robert Howieson (1974-1975) lived in the manse there. There is also a lamp post minus glass on Castle Brae.

The Motor Age
Possibly the greatest changes noticeable in Newport in the last hundred years have been brought about by the arrival of the motor car. Gradually the 'horseless carriage' has taken over. The ferries which had earlier carried carts now transported motor vehicles, businesses which had started as cycle repairers developed into motor

repairers and the blacksmith who had shod horses was finding such traditional skills were hardly needed: to survive in the modern world new skills had to be developed. The empty streets seen in old photographs are very different from those of today, and it was the town council which had to make arrangements and allowances to accommodate this new form of transport.

As early as 1902 the first traffic warning signs were erected, and in 1907 motor cars were limited to a speed of 10 mph within the burgh. This speed limit was still in force in the 1930s and not surprisingly there were frequent reports of speeding. It's interesting to note that we have come almost full circle here, with the speed limit in much of the village having been dropped in recent years to 20 mph. In 1926 the first white guiding lines were painted on the roads at two danger spots – the top of High Street and at 'doctor's corner' on Cupar Road. These proved so successful that the system was adopted elsewhere in the village. Parking soon proved a problem, and in 1931 there were complaints to the council that private cars were being left parked on public streets for hours at a time! These 1930s grumblers might well be silenced if they could see today's situation.

Other attempts at road safety and improvement were attempted. In

Kirk Road before road widening and tree-felling.

1903, it seems that the roads of the burgh were in such a bad condition that a steam roller was purchased. According to letters of William Cowley, roads convenor, this was a great success and the steam roller was then hired out to other towns to do the same job. It steamed as far afield as Crieff. Despite the success of the road roller however, the Town Council in 1912 was receiving complaints from the residents of Cupar Road about the dust nuisance caused by motor traffic which was "resulting in injury to houses and gardens". In 1934, the trees on the High Street, clearly seen in old photographs, were removed to improve visibility for traffic. Inexplicably, the very next year, the trees were re-planted in almost the same places.

Electric street lighting was introduced in the burgh in 1950, a further improvement to safety and convenience. The gas lights which were in use before then had of course all been disused during the black-out of World War II. Inevitably accidents occurred during the black-out and sadly many of the gas lamps which were positioned all the way up Cupar Road as far as the south Tayfield lodge were knocked down. At the time the poor driving of the Polish soldiers who were camped in Tayfield grounds was blamed.

Street Signs
The council put up the first street names as early as 1900, and they reported many more being signposted in 1927. In fact there have been numerous street name changes over the years. Tay Street was known earlier as Tayport Road, and before 1864 as North Street, Maryton. Before the building of the Blyth Hall, Blyth Street was Prinlaws Place: this presumably a reference to the area in mid-Fife where the Berry family had an earlier connection. Albert Crescent was previously Albert Street, Kerr Street until about 1950 was Woodriffe Terrace, and Gas Lane became Granary Lane in 1961. West Newport was even more

confusing than now, with an Upper Woodmuir Terrace (now Beechwood), Woodmuir Terrace and Lower Woodmuir Terrace (now Woodmuir Crescent). West Road was given this name in 1963, but was previously Woodhaven Road and Newburgh Road. Old Kirk Road has now become Kirk Road, so named because it was the route taken by those from West Newport (or the Waterside as it was known earlier) as they headed for the old Forgan Kirk. The re-numbering of the houses in all the streets was done fully and systematically only in 1960 – an arrangement which must have made life easier for the local postmen and delivery boys.

In 1955 the town council made the decision to change the burgh's name to "Newport-on-Tay" (Fife). Until then the official address had been "Newport, Dundee, Angus".

Housing
One of the biggest continuing problems which the town council had to deal with was that of housing. Throughout the 20th century there were frequent reports of houses being unfit for human habitation and orders had to be placed on these buildings to be improved or demolished. If houses were demolished then new houses had to be built, and the council turned their attention to this immediately after the First World War. At that time the government was pressurised to

This 1960s view of the east end of the village shows the pre-fab housing in Kerr Street/Tay Terrace.

provide returning soldiers with 'Homes Fit for Heroes' and several Housing Acts were passed by central government to implement this, encouraging local authorities to provide good quality housing. In 1919 it was decided to build the first council houses at Station Place (Station Brae/Kilgask Street), and these were officially opened with much ceremony in December 1921. These were followed by houses at Woodhaven in 1929 and in Queen Street in the mid 1930s. By 1939 the housing situation had improved greatly, and the sanitary officer's report stated that the burgh's housing problems were "almost entirely solved, with 59 unfit houses being either demolished or repaired".

During the war years, little was done to alleviate any housing problems, and although Newport fortunately did not experience the destruction of housing caused by bombing, by 1945 there was a local housing shortage. Before the war ended however, the town council was already planning its future housing policy. All over the country exhibitions were being held to demonstrate the new factory-made temporary pre-fabricated houses (pre-fabs), and it seemed that these could help satisfy Newport's housing needs. Accordingly, land in Kerr Street and King Street which had previously been used for allotments was now used for pre-fabs, twelve being built at Kerr Street and four in King Street. Ex-residents of the pre-fabs have very fond memories of living there: there was a great community spirit among the residents, with for example regular beetle and whist drives and other social get-togethers being held. These pre-fabs lasted until 1968 when the ground was cleared for re-building, and in the case of Kerr Street sold for private housing.

But in the immediate post-war years, in part due to the 'baby boom' of the late 1940s, still more houses were required: this was a problem experienced nationwide. Thus the council's most ambitious plans were drawn up for 44 houses at Craighead Farm, with more being added a few years later. It was agreed that these houses should have all modern conveniences: cookers, washing machines and refrigerators would be provided. When the pre-fabs in Kerr and King Streets were cleared for demolition, many of the residents were re-housed at Craighead.

In 1955 the council purchased Kinbrae House and grounds, although not initially for the purpose of house-building. Other suggestions for the building's use were put forward and they included a remand home, a hotel, and extra classroom accommodation for the school, at that time very overcrowded. But by 1960 the decision was made not only to build in the grounds, but also to demolish the house. When the Kinbrae Park site was completed, it was considered so successful that visitors from many other local authorities came to view it.

Also in the 1950's Seacraig Court was built. This was on the site of the former Seacraig House and Seacraig Cottages on King Street/Union Street. The Maryton block of flats, its name a reminder of the old village, replaced the King Street pre-fabs and the old police house and cells. The present-day Royal Buildings replaced old buildings on the west side of Robert Street between Tay Street and Union Street. Here, there had been at different times over the years, a hotel and public house (the Royal Hotel), a bake-house with shop, the first telephone exchange (entered from Union Street), and various other businesses and places of refreshment. These buildings are easily recognisable in old photographs by the turret and spire on the Tay Street/Robert Street corner. Finally the area of ground at Albert Crescent which had been used since the Second World War for allotments became in the late 1960s the site of houses for the elderly.

Celebrations

During the years of its existence, the town council had frequently to arrange celebrations of various kinds. Following the death of Queen Victoria in 1901, lavish plans were laid all over Britain to celebrate the coronation in June 1902 of her son Edward VII. Here in Newport plans were equally lavish. A grand fete with games and sports would be held in Waterstone Park. A procession to Waterstone from the Blyth Hall would be made up of the town council, the parish council, the school board, boys from the Mars, Newport School, Miss Wayman's School and Newport BB. Children from Wormit and Forgan Schools and from Comerton Home would make separate processions to the park. All the children involved would receive gifts of sweets and commemorative medals. Commemorative iron seats would be placed throughout the burgh, and two bonfires would be lit. A gold chain was acquired for the Provost, and a halberd with the burgh arms on it was gifted to the burgh by Provost Thomson.

One can only imagine the shock, concern and disappointment when just two days before the Coronation news came that the ceremony had been cancelled as the king had to undergo emergency surgery. Fortunately his speedy recovery allowed the celebrations to go ahead in August instead.

In 1911 George V's coronation was celebrated with the opening of the new Windmill Park. This park would serve the village until it was cut off by the building of the access road to the new road bridge in the 1960s. A ceremonial gold key was used for the opening and presented to Provost and Mrs Robertson by the contractors. Some thirty years later this key would be presented to the council by the Robertson family for safekeeping. Newport enjoyed a day of processions, sports and games in the new park.

George V and Mary celebrated their Silver Jubilee in 1935, and the occasion was marked, not only by the usual village sports and processions, but also by the presentation from Buckingham Palace of Jubilee medals to Provost Scrymgeour and Town Clerk Frank Morrison. Mr Morrison incidentally held this post for 37 years and on his retiral in 1953 was given the freedom of Newport and made the first Honorary Burgess of the burgh. The only other person to receive this honour was Miss Maude Pilkington in 1970 in recognition of her service to the community.

1937 gave further cause for celebration, first of all with the coronation of King George VI, king rather suddenly and unexpectedly after his brother Edward's abdication. A fancy dress parade for both children and vehicles led to Windmill Park where new swings and play apparatus were provided. At night there was a concert and bonfire, and children and the elderly were given commemorative gifts. In October of that year, Newport celebrated its own Golden Jubilee – 50 years of being a burgh. A dinner and a dance were held in the Blyth Hall, and a party for 300 children.

We are fortunate that these celebrations of 1935 and 1937 were recorded on cine film by the Lawson family of Balmore. The film has been transferred and updated first to video then to DVD, and has been viewed and enjoyed by hundreds of visitors to Old Newport exhibitions. The coronation of our present Queen Elizabeth was celebrated in 1953, when there were the usual procession to Windmill Park, decoration of streets and the distribution of gifts to the schoolchildren. This great event provided for many people the first experience of watching television! Many of the villagers saw it on sets positioned in the Blyth Hall and in the school fitted up by local electrician James Fairlie.

Royal Visits

The Brownies greet the royal visitor in 1950. Brown Owl Nancy French in the centre.

Three times since the end of the Second World War Newport has enjoyed royal visits.

In 1950 the Queen (the wife of King George VI, later the Queen Mother) passed through the village en route

Queen Elizabeth, later the Queen Mother, is greeted on the High Street by Provost Lawson.

from Newburgh and stopped to meet local people. A welcome platform was set up on the High street where Provost Lawson and other local dignitaries waited to greet her. She was presented with an Address of Welcome which had been designed by Mr Haeburn-Little of Kilnburn. In June 1958 the present Queen and Prince Philip visited the village as part of their tour of Fife. Busloads of sightseers arrived in the village, and hundreds more crossed from Dundee by ferry. Once again a platform was set up on the High

Street, and the Provosts of Newport and Tayport along with other local dignitaries paraded from the burgh chambers to the High Street. The procession was led by the burgh officer carrying his halberd. Gifts for the royal children, Charles and Anne, then aged ten and eight, were presented to the Queen. The Queen and Prince Philip departed from the pier in the royal barge to join the Royal Yacht Britannia, moored out in the river off East Newport. In 1966 the Queen Mother returned, not quite to Newport itself, but to open the new road bridge. Crowds awaited her arrival at the Newport end of the bridge, as she drove across in an open top car.

Later Local Government Re-organisation

1975 sadly saw the end of Newport Town Council and other similar local town councils across Scotland. To mark such a significant end to this chapter in Newport's life an "End of Burgh Ceremony" was held in the Blyth Hall. Presentations were made to three officials: Mr Alex Gilruth, town clerk for 28 years; Mr Jack Morton, burgh surveyor for 27 years; and Mr Ian Clark, burgh chamberlain. Provost Rev. Robert Howieson paid tribute to all those who had served the burgh in the previous years.

The local government reorganisation of that year saw the implementation of the 1973 Local Government

(Scotland) Act which abolished previous existing local government structures and created a two-tier system of regions and districts. Newport would be governed at a local level by North East Fife District Council and at a county level by Fife Council. The path towards this had not been straightforward as the original plans had envisaged Fife being carved in three, with Tayport, Newport, Wormit, Gauldry and Balmerino being included in Tayside region. An energetic campaign was launched to preserve Fife as one region and this was successful. Newport became part of North East Fife District Council area, in turn part of Fife region, until further local government reorganisation in 1994.

The Local Government Act of 1994 abolished the two-tier structure of districts and regions, and instead Scotland was divided into thirty-two unitary authorities. This time there was no question of splitting Fife: it would remain a single area, and today Newport still comes under Fife Council jurisdiction.

Provosts of the Burgh of Newport-on-Tay

1887-96	Alexander Scott	Ashbank Villa, 70 Tay Street
1896-99	Andrew Leitch	Netherlea, 65 West Road
1899-02	Alexander Thomson	Ravensby, 14 Norwood
1902-05	Thomas Roger	Snowdon, 16 Tay Terrace
1905-08	William Carswell	Ascot, 3 Beechwood Terrace
1908-11	William Robertson	Struan Bank, 26 Birkhill Avenue, Wormit
1911-14	Robert Thomson Leitch	Hillcrest, 5 Wellpark Terrace West
1914-19	Simon Forrest	Craigard, 108 Tay Street
1919-22	James Coutts	Clifton, 31 Riverside Road, Wormit
1922-25	Charles William Buik	Braeknowe, 9 Wellpark Terrace West
1925-28	James Barry Robb	Whinhurst, 10 Crosshill Terrace, Wormit
1928-31	William Forrest French	Taybank, 2 Tay Street
1931-34	John Thomson Young	Linwood, 28 Linden Avenue
1934-37	George Scrymgeour	Cadzow, 14 Kirk Road
1937-40	George Rain Little	Taybank, 59 Bay Road, Wormit
1940-43	Frank Howard Fairweather	4 Struan Place
1943-46	Kenneth C Hayens	Woodlea, 25 Westfield Terrace
1946-50	J D M Ross	4 Hill Crescent, Wormit
1950-52	J Douglas Lawson	Balmore, Newburgh Road
1952-55	John Dunn	Rowan Bank, 7 Riverside Road, Wormit
1955-57	Richard Lowry West	Craighead House, 94 Tay Street
1957-60	Thomas J Wishart	Fernbrae, 56 Riverside Road, Wormit
1960-63	Alex D Forrest	Arnsheen, Westfield Terrace
1963-65	A C Newell	8 Prospect Terrace
1965-68	William J Smith	Westlea, 65 Bay Road, Wormit
1968-71	J Gordon Soutar	Westcroft, 12 Kilmany Road, Wormit
1971-74	Randolph Webster	7 Woodmuir Crescent
1974-75	Robert A Howieson	The Manse, Blyth Street

TAY ROAD BRIDGE

The ferries which had crossed the river from early times had served the village well, but as road traffic increased in the twentieth century, the idea of building a road bridge across the Tay began to attract a strong following. At the beginning of the twentieth century however the railways continued to carry most of the country's passengers and freight and it seemed then as if a road bridge would be an expensive and unjustifiable luxury. Only when it became clear that the motor car was indeed the transport of the future did the idea of a road bridge become acceptable. By the mid 1920s the Government hinted strongly that they would be prepared to give financial support to the construction of a bridge. Agreements were reached with the Government and the local councils of Fife, Angus and Dundee as to their respective contributions. Test bores were carried out and a bridge design chosen. Sadly however economic circumstances intervened and the Depression of the late 1920s and 1930s left neither the Government nor Dundee in any position to pursue such an ambitious project and plans were dropped.

Six years of war necessarily shelved the enterprise, and in the immediate post-war years more urgent problems required attention. In the 1950s an energetic campaign was launched in Dundee and raised public awareness of the need and desire for a bridge. A Tay Road Bridge Joint Committee was formed in 1955. The campaign gathered momentum: petitions were signed, traffic censuses were carried out and money was raised. Further test bores showed the feasibility of a bridge. William Fairhurst was chosen as project engineer and in 1960 his plans were accepted by the Bridge Committee. In 1961 the Government agreed to the bridge construction.

The Government however made it clear from the beginning that it would support the bridge only if all building and running costs were met by tolls. Reluctantly the Committee accepted this, and it was agreed that the three local authorities, Dundee, Fife and Angus, would each contribute to the building costs of the bridge, with the Government advancing the remainder. All money lent would be repaid in due course, if necessary over 60 years. Scottish Government legislation would eventually scrap the tolls, this taking effect in 2008.

The Committee, having set things in motion, became, with a few changes, the Tay Road Bridge Joint Board. It was this body which controlled the building of the bridge and which still controls the running of it.

Building the Bridge

Fairhurst's design was for a bridge of forty-two concrete and steel spans. Steel box girders would be supported on concrete columns. The bridge would rise steadily from a height of 20 feet at Dundee to 125 feet at the Fife landfall. The design of the columns was masterful: the double parabolic shape was unique and stylish, and meant that each column looked good regardless of height. As the bridge rose towards the Fife shore the gradient was a constant 1 in 81 for the whole length. The increased height at the Fife side meant that the shipping channel could be accommodated just where the water was deepest and the bridge was of a sufficient height.

This view of the temporary bridge shows the coffer dams which were dug down into the river bed. Each coffer dam would eventually accommodate one pillar.

Landfall on the Fife side.

119

Although the spans look of equal length across the entire length of the bridge this is not the case. Fairhurst allowed for perspective and the action of the human eye by making the central spans considerably longer than those closer to shore. Fairhurst's original design allowed for 3 carriageways and a pedestrian path on either side. By putting one pedestrian pathway along the middle enough money was saved to allow for four carriageways. Viewing platforms were installed over the toll booths at the Dundee end of the bridge and over the shipping channel to allow pedestrians uninterrupted views of the bridge and river.

Once the design was finalised tenders for the work were invited, and the firm of Duncan Logan was chosen. Headed by Willie Duncan this firm had an impressive reputation.

Work began on 29th March 1963. Instead of building the bridge from barges as was the norm, Logan and Fairhurst had agreed that a more efficient system would be to build a temporary low level bridge as a base from which to build the main bridge. This would allow easy transportation of materials and

This view illustrates the massive disruption at the Fife abutment.
Progress on new road system in the background.

Construction of the new dual carriageway behind Norwood.

would allow work to continue even in bad weather. Although initially costly to build, it should in the long run save money. Once the temporary bridge had advanced some way into the river, then erection of the first columns could begin. Slowly the bridge crept southwards, the uniquely designed columns rising higher and higher. A milestone in the bridge construction was achieved on 15th February 1965 as Lord Provost McManus of Dundee shook hands with Provost William Smith of Newport on the closing of the final gap in the temporary bridge. Fife and Angus were at last linked.

During construction there was considerable upheaval at both ends of the bridge as new access roads were constructed. In Dundee this involved the infilling of the Earl Grey dock, as well as the demolition of much loved landmarks the Royal Arch and Dundee West Station.

At the Fife end of the bridge there was massive disruption and change to the landscape immediately to the south. A new road was driven from the bridge to meet the old A914 near the Sandford Hotel. Massive rock blasting was involved near the bridge as the dual carriageway was driven through the hill behind

This section of the new road severed the railway line to Tayport.

Newport, and residents of houses nearby recall a frightening instance of rocks landing in their gardens. The building of this dual carriageway necessitated slicing through the railway line to Tayport in May 1966. For three months until the opening of the bridge in August rail passengers to Tayport were taken from Newport to Tayport by bus. Thereafter their only transport option was by road and bridge. Also affected by the building of the dual carriageway was the St Fort estate, split in two by the new road. And above Newport the Windmill Park was cut off from the village and no longer easily accessible.

Not only on land did the bridge construction cause disruption. The ferries too were affected. At times of low tides, the ferries had to swing away downstream to avoid the sandbank in the middle of the river. Once the temporary bridge was completed the ferries had no room to manoeuvre and sailings at low tide had to be cancelled. For long periods in the day, for anything up to six hours, there was no ferry service. On one occasion the Abercraig suffered engine failure and was driven by wind against the temporary bridge. Some damage was suffered by both the boat and bridge, and passengers had to be led

Some of the first vehicles on the first section of the dual carriageway.

to safety along the temporary bridge in gale force winds.

The Bridge in Operation

Finally, by the summer of 1966, the bridge was completed. It was opened on Thursday 18th August by Queen Elizabeth the Queen Mother. After the official opening ceremony in Dundee, the royal party, led by a police car, drove slowly over the new bridge and a flag-waving crowd awaited the royal visitor at the Fife end of the bridge. The Queen Mother was greeted by John McWilliam Lord Lieutenant of Fife and presented with a bouquet by Susan Smith, daughter of Newport Provost William Smith. Celebrations were held in Newport after the

bridge was opened, with a fancy dress procession then a gala in Tayfield grounds, where Provost Smith and the Convenor of Fife Council planted two trees to mark the occasion.

The bridge had taken three and a half years to build and cost £4.8 million. At the time of construction it was, at 7265 feet or 1.4 miles, the longest road bridge in Britain and the fifth longest in Europe. Sadly contractor Willie Logan never saw his bridge completed. He was killed in January 1966 when the plane he was piloting crashed near Inverness. His gravestone in Fodderty cemetery, near Strathpeffer, is in the shape of a section of the Tay Road Bridge. At a peak three hundred and

Burgh of Newport-on-Tay

The Provost, Magistrates & Councillors authorise the admission of the Bearer to the Enclosed Area at the South end of the Bridge in Newport-on-Tay on the occasion of the opening of the Tay Road Bridge.

on Thursday, 18th August, 1966

by Her Majesty, Queen Elizabeth The Queen Mother

Guests must be seated by 11.30 a.m.

Invitation to the bridge opening ceremony.

sixty men worked on the bridge construction. Five were killed, two falling from the bridge and three when a section of the temporary bridge fell in the river. The tall column in the centre of the roundabout at the south end of the bridge, shaped like a bridge column, is a memorial to these five workers and to Willie Logan. There is a smaller memorial of similar design on the Dundee shore.

As agreed before construction, tolls would be charged for those using the bridge. In 1966 the toll for cars was 2/6 (12½p), for motor cycles 1/- (10p) and for heavy goods vehicles 10/- (50p). Cyclists travelled free but until the 1990s would share the main roadway with motor vehicles. The central walkway was for pedestrians only. Toll booths for collection of tolls both north- and south-bound were positioned on a wide plaza at the north end of the bridge. Toll collection would eventually cause considerable congestion and queuing at peak times of the day.

Indeed in the late 1980s when road works on the bridge aggravated the congestion, at morning rush hour the north-bound queue tailed down

The Queen Mother at the Fife end of the bridge with Mr John McWilliam, County Convener and Lord Lieutenant of Fife.

on to, and along, Tay Street in Newport.

In 1966 it was predicted that some 3000 cars per day would use the bridge, and that this figure would rise to 10,000 within ten years. By the following year 6,000 cars were crossing each day and by 1992 the figure had risen to 20,000. Now in 2015 25,000 vehicles cross daily.

In 1989 the toll was increased from 12½p to 30p, and in 1992 to 80p one way. One-way tolling had been introduced the previous year in order to cut down on north-bound congestion at peak times. This had proved very successful.

In 2007 the Scottish Government voted to abolish tolls on the Forth and Tay bridges. This took effect the following year and the toll booths were removed soon afterwards.

Certain changes have been made to improve safety on the bridge. The viewing platforms were removed, with the one above the toll collection booths being removed in 1988. In 1998 the central viewing platform was removed as part of a major refurbishment of the central walkway. At this time it was also decided that cyclists were at risk

The old observation platform in the middle of the bridge,
much appreciated for its fine views up and down river.

when using the main carriageways and should therefore use the central walkway instead. A lift was installed at the Dundee end of the bridge to allow them access to the walkway, and steps at the south end were converted to a ramp.

Without doubt the opening of the Tay Road Bridge in 1966 opened a new chapter in the story of Newport. Certainly the end of the ferry service signalled the end of an era. The building of the bridge was viewed with dismay and apprehension by some villagers, as it seemed that it must make Newport altogether too accessible to Dundee and to the outside world. This fear however turned out to be largely unfounded. Certainly the journey between Dundee and Fife became simpler (if somewhat less friendly and more anonymous), but it was perhaps the parts of Fife beyond Newport which really became more accessible to Dundee. After all Newport and Dundee had always been closely linked by the ferries. Undoubtedly the village saw huge changes in the second half of the twentieth century, but perhaps no more as a result of building the road bridge than of general progress. Newport appears to have suffered less by the march of

The toll plaza at north end of bridge, after one-way tolling had been adopted.
The multi-storey flats on skyline are now also gone.

so-called progress than many similar communities, and still manages to retain its own identity, community spirit and friendly village character.

NEWPORT AT WAR

Twice in the twentieth century Newport played its part in world wars, with young men of the village departing to serve their country and, as the war memorial testifies, in too many cases not returning. Both in the first and second wars evidence of the conflict was apparent in the community.

Boer War memorial in the Leng Chapel.

Even before these two great struggles, Newport's young men had been serving their country in various conflicts. For example in the South African Boer War of 1899-1902, six local lads volunteered for the army. They left from Newport station where station-master James Duncan kindly and optimistically gave them all return tickets. Sadly his kindness and optimism were to no avail, as only one of the volunteers returned. The names of the five lost are commemorated on a

HMS Vulcan and its attendant submarines.

128

plaque in the Leng Chapel at Vicarsford cemetery.

> Private Alexander Kidd
> – aged 23
> Private Alfred Mathewson
> – aged 21
> Private John Turnbull
> – aged 21
> Private Joseph Hopton
> – aged 21
> Private Alexander Fairweather
> – aged 22

As naval tension with Germany increased in the years before World War I, in 1909 the Admiralty took out a 5 year lease of part of Dundee harbour as a shore base for a North Sea submarine flotilla. Dundee was chosen because of its graving dock, shore facilities and the fact that the River Tay was a tricky one for enemy craft to navigate.

Newport afforded a good anchorage for the submarines and for HMS Vulcan, the repair ship attached to the flotilla. Vulcan, nine submarines and two torpedo destroyers were based here.

By the time the lease had run out, World War I had started, and the building of the Rosyth Naval Base on the Forth resulted in the submarines moving there.

World War One

During the First World War large numbers of troops in training were stationed in Wormit. Between 400 and 500 were billeted firstly in houses, and later in the large camp which was erected at Highfield.

Highland Light Infantry camp at Highfield, Wormit in 1917.

Sixteen huts were built, as well as a hospital, stores, a cookhouse, latrines, bathrooms and a recreation hall. The new Windmill Park behind Newport was also occupied by the military, with a searchlight and huts installed, and trenches dug to simulate as closely as possible the conditions the soldiers would encounter when at the front. The Highland Light Infantry drilled there, and provided much entertainment for local boys, who irreverently referred to them as BLH – Britain's Last Hope. The YMCA set up a canteen for soldiers in the Blyth Hall. There were mixed feelings on this, as there were complaints to the council about soldiers causing a nuisance in St Mary's Lane.

After the war, captured German guns stood for several years outside the Blyth Hall. The first plan for a war memorial was actually for an artistic entrance porch to the hall, but the present memorial, on its site overlooking the river, was unveiled in September 1922, after an alternative site at the top of Kilnburn steps had been rejected. The memorial was designed by Robert Lorimer, designer of the National War Memorial in Edinburgh Castle. It was unveiled in September 1922 by Sir Ralph Anstruther, Lord Lieutenant of Fife.

Stop and examine the eighty-four names on the memorial, eighty-four names from such a small village. There are many you will recognise

as belonging to families still in Newport today. Look for the name of Peter Black, the young man whose name almost didn't appear.

The recently unveiled war memorial in 1922.

Peter joined the army as soon as World War I broke out and, like so many others from this area, served in the Black Watch. During fierce fighting in 1915, he suffered from shell shock and was severely disturbed. He then experienced further fierce fighting in the Somme area in 1916, and at that point his nerve finally cracked and he deserted. Sadly, in the armies of World War I, there was no place for deserters, and as punishment and as an example to others, like 305 others, Peter was shot by firing squad in September 1916.

The grave of Peter Black in Les Trois Arbres cemetery in France.

When the authorities were arranging the erection of the war memorial in Newport, local people, including many young men who had fought with Peter, were outraged to learn that as a deserter his name would be excluded. Explosives were stolen from a local quarry and hidden in a house in Robert Street (No. 13) and threats to blow up the memorial were made unless Peter's name was included. His name was added, and the explosives found their way back to the quarry.

In 2006 it was at last announced by the Government that all 306 of the First World War soldiers who were shot for cowardice or desertion would be granted a posthumous pardon.

For many years, I visited the battlefields and cemeteries of World War I in Belgium and France with pupils from Bell Baxter High School in Cupar, on their annual study visit. It was a very special moment for me when we were able to track down and visit Peter's grave in Les Trois Arbres cemetery in northern France. I have visited on many occasions since, always leaving a poppy cross and remembering that young man, but never seeing any indication of any other visitors.

World War Two

By the time the Second World War broke out on 3rd September 1939, preparations for it were already underway. Between 1936 and 1939 the Spanish Civil War had demonstrated all too clearly the horrors of a modern war, and the Munich crisis of September 1938 had brought Britain so close to war, that plans for evacuation and air raid precautions had been drawn up at that time.

Gas and Air Raid Precautions

Perhaps the greatest fear was that of gas attacks, and the village's consignment of gas masks arrived at the time of the Munich crisis in 1938. The babies' ones arrived later. These were large bulky affairs, into which the babies fitted almost completely, with just their little legs dangling free! One of these can be seen in the heritage room in Newport library. Air raid wardens were equipped with football rattles, to be used only to warn of the presence of poison gas. Everyone was supposed to carry their gas mask everywhere, neatly fitted in its brown cardboard box. Regular gas mask practices were held, especially in schools and work places. Some ex-pupils can still recall chanting their times tables through their gas masks.

In order to ensure that local residents knew what precautions to take in the event of air raids, an Air Raid Precautions headquarters was set up in King Street – in a house which incidentally had already been declared unfit for human habitation. One of the first tasks for those who had volunteered for ARP duty was to ensure that black-out regulations were followed, and practices for this were carried out throughout 1939. No outside lights were permitted at all. How strange it must have been to look out across the river to Dundee in utter darkness. In fact the black-out was so absolute that on one occasion during the war, when a rogue light showed in Robert Street, the ferry master took it to be the permitted guiding light on the pier. The result was one stranded ferry on the beach at the foot of the Braes. A more tragic incident occurred when a Dundee worker at the Steele and Brodie beehive works in Wormit stepped to his death from a stationary train on the Tay Bridge, believing he had arrived in the blacked-out Wormit station. The accident was all the more tragic as the man had been making the same journey for twenty-two years.

The air raid siren was fitted on the front of the Blyth Hall. To begin with there were complaints that it could not be heard in West Newport and Wormit, and one was later fitted on Wormit School.

Soon after the war started it was decided that four public air raid shelters should be built: at Gas Lane (now area of Granary Lane), in King Street, in the garden of Broadheugh on West Road, and in Wormit next to Fife House. In addition to these, part of John T Young's garage on Boat Road was offered as a convenient shelter for passengers from the ferry. Newport School had its own air raid shelters, at the top of the playground below the Scott Street wall. Wormit School however at first had to make other arrangements. The school log book describes an air raid practice in 1939. Children who lived within seven minutes of the school were sent home. All other children lay on the floor of their classroom under the desks. How safe that would have been is doubtful. Eventually two air raid shelters were built in the Wormit School field.

Local residents were also

Air raid shelter sign with Kinbrae House in background.

a raid on Dundee or Aberdeen saw a light and dropped perhaps its last bomb. Apparently the light was from a lantern used by someone visiting the outside toilet. The cottage suffered considerable damage and the windows in nearby Chesterhill House and Lodge were broken. The toilet user was only slightly injured. In 1942 all our unwanted shelters were despatched to Worthing in Sussex, where presumably the need and desire for shelter were greater!

Evacuation and Evacuees

Although the first planned evacuation of children and other vulnerable groups from danger areas had been planned a year earlier, the first evacuated children arrived in the village on Friday, 1st September 1939, the day which saw the start of the mass exodus from cities all over Britain. In the spring of 1939 it had been decided that Newport would be able to accommodate a staggering total of 3762 evacuees – fortunately nowhere near that number ever appeared! Others followed throughout the war, mainly from Edinburgh and Glasgow. They were usually taken to Kirk House first (this was the church hall of St Thomas' Church, situated upstairs from the Cupar Road row of shops), then allocated to families and sent out to homes from there. Sometimes the totally unexpected happened. On one occasion a train-

encouraged to make their own shelters, and the town council assisted with advice and materials for these. In 1941 a supply of Morrison and Anderson shelters arrived in the village. For those with a garden the corrugated iron and curved roofed Anderson shelters were dug into the ground. Even today they can still be seen being used as garden sheds, especially on allotment sites. The Morrison shelter was for use indoors and was rather like a very large metal table with mesh sides. By 1941 however the people of Newport were perhaps becoming somewhat blasé, and there was no great rush to accept the shelters. In fact the only bomb which fell on or near the village during the war landed in November 1940 near Washer Willy's cottage on the Inverdovat road. It's understood that a lone German plane returning from load of 80 boys was due to arrive from Southbridge, one of Edinburgh's less salubrious areas. All was ready for them, and foster parents, although fairly reluctant, had been found for the boys. The train did arrive, but carried no boys from Southbridge, who had apparently disappeared off somewhere into the depths of Angus – no-one quite knew where. And Newport's new arrivals? The expectant mothers instead! Many of them had their babies while staying here.

From the minutes of the town council it appears that there was much resistance in the village towards evacuation. By 1940 the council decreed that the village could only support 600 evacuees, and then only under compulsion. To help with accommodation, Rolleston on Cupar Road was rented as a hostel for evacuees, Dr William Leng generously offering to pay rent and rates. This worked well for a time but it was unfortunately forced to close in 1942 due to a shortage of domestic help, a common problem during the war. Many of the local girls had either joined the forces, or had found new employment and much higher wages in the munitions factories in Dundee. Thereafter the house was taken over by the Department of Agriculture as accommodation for the Land Army girls who helped out on local farms. There was also a canteen organised

in the Congregational Church hall at the bottom of Kilnburn, no longer there, where the evacuees might have their mid-day meal. It too was short-lived as it was taken over by, and for, the military. It had however been the first of its kind in Scotland. By the end of the war, perhaps as a result of the luke-warm welcome extended to them combined with the greater safety of the cities, only three evacuee families remained in Newport. Within a year of the ending of the war, they too had left.

Threat of Invasion
Throughout the war years the village had to maintain a high degree of readiness in case of attack. After the fall of Norway in 1940 the threat of invasion from that direction towards the east coast of Scotland became a real likelihood. Defences all along the east coast were intensified. The remains of concrete defences can still be seen along the beaches at Tayport and Tentsmuir, and posts were erected in flat fields to hinder airborne glider invasion. As in other towns and villages the Home Guard was set up, under the leadership of Alex Lowson. They were based in the ARP building in King Street and drilled and practised in Windmill Park, again no doubt providing much entertainment for local youngsters. In Wormit, the Home Guard was based in the shops on Riverside Road. Successful invasion exercises were held and the

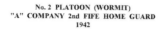

No. 2 PLATOON (WORMIT)
"A" COMPANY 2nd FIFE HOME GUARD
1942

Back Row - J. Bryce, R. Wannan, W. Duncan, D. Tanner, A. Fox, W. Carswell, C. Robertson, C. Minns
2nd Back Row - C. Porter, J. Doughty, A. Robertson, W. Neakes, T. Elder, J. Baird, A. Clark, R. Young, A. Dowie
Middle Row - D. Stewart, F. Robertson, J. Jeffrey, A. Smith, S. Bisset, G. Noakes
2nd Front Row - L/Cpl. D. Cargill, L/Cpl. J. Howie, Cpl. A. Wannan, Cpl. E. McDonald, Cpl. J. Pringle, L/Cpl. A. Fraser, L/Cpl. J. Ireland
Front Row - Sgt. J. Duncan, Sgt. W. Kidd, 2nd/Lieut. J. Lillie, Lieut. E. Hope, M.C., L/Cpl. D. Cowley

Wormit Home Guard pictured outside their base in two of the shops.

sanitary inspector issued detailed instructions on the supply of drinking water and disposal of waste in the event of an attack. Church bells were silenced and would only be rung as an invasion alarm. Most households were prepared for fire with stirrup-pumps and sand buckets, and there were extra water tanks for fire-fighting positioned at Kirk Road and in Wormit. All house lofts were to be cleared to reduce the risk of fire – no easy task. The Blyth Hall was fitted out as a first aid post, and in the event of an attack with resultant casualties then the school next door would be used as a rest centre. This caused much amusement among pupils who remarked that many had been treating it as such for some considerable time anyway! Local farmers had to ensure that their hay stacks had extra space between them in case of incendiary bombs.

There was a strong military presence both in and around the village. Polish soldiers camped in Tayfield until 1942. Interestingly these Polish soldiers actually wore tartan patches on their upper arms. This was nothing to do with their training in

Scotland, but allegedly because they came from the area of Poland associated with Bonnie Prince Charlie. Bonnie Prince Charlie's mother was a grand-daughter of the Polish King John Sobieski. On one occasion the Polish troops in Tayfield were inspected by no less a personage than General Sikorski, Prime Minister of the Polish government in exile, and Commander-in-Chief of the Polish armed forces. As a gesture of welcome to the Polish soldiers, any who wished were invited to be honorary members of Newport Tennis Club.

A dummy airfield at St. Michaels, designed to divert enemy attention from Leuchars airfield, provided more military personnel. A forces canteen was organised in the Trinity Church hall for the entertainment of the troops, and all the local churches took turns at catering. Concerts were held in the Rio Cinema, newly opened when war broke out, the entertainment sometimes being provided by the Polish soldiers or by the Home Guard. On a more basic note, showers fitted in the Blyth Hall for first aid were soon being used by 100 soldiers per day.

The Norwegians at Woodhaven

After the German occupation of Norway in the spring of 1940, Norwegian civilians and forces personnel fought a resistance war both within and from outside Norway. From February 1942 onwards Norwegian forces were based at Woodhaven after the 333 squadron of the Royal Norwegian Air Force was formed there in 1942. Woodhaven was chosen as the squadron's base because of its relatively isolated location which offered the secrecy needed for its missions. The pier was used to service the squadron's Catalina flying boats which would soon become a familiar sight on the Tay. The Norwegians flew their Catalinas on sorties out over the North Sea and into enemy occupied Norway. For much of 1942 and 1943 they regularly dropped spies in Norway and, even more dangerous, had the task of picking them up again. On a lighter note, at Christmas 1942 they dropped 52 sacks of food and Christmas presents. In addition the Catalinas were used for anti-submarine work, reconnaissance flights over the north Atlantic and escort duties for the Allied Arctic convoys, often patrolling ahead to check on ice conditions.

Access to the pier at that time was forbidden to the public, with a sentry box at the top of both approach roads. While the Norwegians were there they received a rather unexpected 'visitor'. Local people were somewhat surprised, and no doubt more than a little alarmed, when one day a German Heinkel seaplane was spotted flying low up the river. It

No entry to Woodhaven pier during the war.

A Catalina flying boat at Woodhaven.

Woodhaven pier – a scene of much activity here, both on- and off-shore.

landed at Woodhaven, but within half an hour, the German markings were painted out. This was no invasion, nor a Rudolf Hess-type mission. This was a German plane appropriated by two Norwegian resistance fighters and flown from Norway to freedom.

Ron Caird remembers as a young boy hearing the Catalinas return from missions at dead of night and, slipping out of bed, watched from his window as they just cleared the spire of St Fillan's Church.

Before the war Woodhaven pier had been used by air force reservists. They camped each year near Inverdovat farm and used the pier at Woodhaven for exercises on their Singapore biplane flying boats.

The Home Front

For six years the war was fought on the home front too as housewives struggled to cope with food rationing, introduced in January 1940 but planned years before, and with other shortages of basic items caused by war. As much food as possible had to be produced at home and so the country was encouraged to "Dig for Victory". For this reason more allotments were provided on the land between Albert Crescent and Youngsdale Place at the expense of the putting green which was located there. The Wormit Bay Golf Club which had been in existence

Provost Fairweather inspects the naval cadets on Kilnburn during Warships Week in 1942.

since 1912, found its land returned to the local farmers to plough up to help with food production. Despite the food shortages during the war people generally ate more healthily when food was rationed: by the end of the war the nation was healthier than it had ever been.

All sorts of goods had to be salvaged. Paper and wool could be re-used, bones could provide cordite for gun cartridges and aluminium and other metals could be melted down to be used for tanks or aeroplanes. The Make Do and Mend campaign encouraged people not to waste anything. Woollen jumpers could be ripped out and re-knitted, or large garments could be made into smaller ones. Many a wartime bride's wedding dress was made

from a length of souvenir parachute silk. Very often bins were positioned at street ends for depositing bones, old aluminium saucepans, or any of the other requested materials. Almost nothing was wasted or discarded. To begin with the salvage collections in Newport and surrounding area were enthusiastically carried out by the school pupils and boy scouts. In 1944, perhaps when enthusiasm was waning, a salvage competition between Newport and Tayport was organised...... Newport won! Certainly it seems that we could learn some recycling lessons today from the salvage experts of the 1940s.

Perhaps one of the most obvious examples of salvage collection was the removal of railings from houses and public buildings. The first request for railings came from the government in 1940. To begin with the town council was very unwilling to consent to this, but more persistent demands from the Ministry of Works followed. In 1942 a survey was carried out, on all gates and railings which could be removed. The council reluctantly agreed to their removal, and work started in March 1943. The many iron-stubbed walls around the village testify to the fact that Newport gave more than average. There is considerable doubt over whether the metal collected in this way was in fact ever used.

Peace Declared

By the time the bonfires were lit in 1945 to celebrate peace, the community could feel that it had made a fair contribution to the war effort, and was more than ready for peace. VE (Victory in Europe) day was declared on Tuesday 8th May, and on the following Sunday thanksgiving services were held in village churches. Fighting would continue in the Far East for a further three months. A further forty-four names of young Newport men had to be added to the war memorial, and it was decided that these would be put on bronze plaques on the low walls facing the memorial.

NEWPORT AT WORK

Newport's development as a residential area has meant that there has been no industrial development here. There are however several local trades and businesses which are worth mentioning, some for their longevity, some for being quite unusual and some probably long forgotten. The following are reminders of some of them. I apologise for omitting any others which may well also be of interest.

Bee Equipment

Steele and Brodie were for most of the twentieth century the only bee equipment manufacturers in Scotland. Robert Steel started his beehive manufacturing in the 1870s in Dundee, and very soon moved to premises in Gauldry. A fire in 1899 forced another move, this time to Kilmany Road, Wormit. Very briefly in 1900 the firm was listed as Steel and Raitt, but thereafter only Robert Steel. By 1910 the more familiar Steele (with an e) and Brodie partnership had evolved, and this partnership soon became a familiar and well respected name among

Steele and Brodie beehive works, Wormit.

beekeepers. After the First World War the company expanded into general joinery work and production of poultry houses, but soon the demand for bee equipment led to their concentration on that. They remained in business as bee equipment manufacturers and suppliers until closure in 1998. Housing now occupies the site of the beehive works, with a decorative panel built into the entrance wall now the only reminder of this once thriving business.

Blacksmiths

In Newport the name John Don is immediately associated with blacksmiths. The Don family came to Newport in the 1870s. Father

James was a gardener, and two of his sons, John J and James jun., became blacksmiths. The family lived in the block of flats which eventually became the site of the Rio Cinema. In the 1880s John J Don's first job was as a rivet boy on the construction of the railway bridge, after which he spent some time making golf clubs in St Andrews. By the mid-1890s he had established blacksmith premises on Victoria Street, roughly where the surgery is today. Much of his work in these early years was sharpening the stonemasons' tools. The house-building boom in Newport and Wormit at the end of the nineteenth century meant the masons' skills were in great demand, and their tools usually had to be sharpened by

Early 1900s view of the pier smiddy and the blacksmiths.

night, ready for the next day. John J would work long into the night, working by candle light and the light from the smiddy fire. In 1909 he moved his business to the smiddy opposite the pier, which had previously been tenanted by Willie Young, father of John T Young who would eventually develop his garage business on Boat Road. John J Don was joined by his son John B in the 1920s. When the pierhead smiddy closed in the 1940s the business moved to premises near the old pier. Soon after this move, grandson John S Don joined the business in the late 1940s and a further move took them to premises in King Street. Finally in the 1980s the business moved to their present location in Naughton Road, Wormit, originally the site of Collie's garage from the early 1900s until the mid-1960s (see Garages below). John S Don's son Brian and grandson Mark continue the business today with John S still taking a close interest in it. In total there have been five generations of Don blacksmiths in the village.

Until the 1880s there was also the Tayfield Smiddy which stood at the junction of Victoria Street and Cupar Road, where Darvel Lodge now stands. The last blacksmiths at the Tayfield smiddy before it closed were William Lowden and his son William.

Just outside the village, on the St Andrews road, was the Forgan smiddy. Originally the smiddy for the St Fort estate it sometimes bore that name. From the 1840s until the 1870s the smiddy was worked by father and son David and John Murdoch, and then until 1926 by Thomas Fearn. In 1926 it was taken over by Kenneth Cunningham who was joined in the 1940s by his son Ken. Ken later developed the business into a successful motor engineering operation.

Carpet Beating

Much less well known was the carpet beating factory in Wormit. This was down Bay Road just before the railway bridge, on the left side of the road (see photograph on page 37). In front of the factory was a large stretch of grass. The earliest mention I could find was in the burgh minutes of 1911-1912 when complaints had been received about dust from the factory blowing over surrounding houses. This problem had been resolved by the installation of a chute to trap and remove the dust to ground level. In 1929 the business was taken over by Harry Johnston, a joiner and funeral director in Wormit. Ron Caird helped out in the factory as a young lad at the end of the war and remembers the enormous carpets being collected by car and trailer from the large houses in Newport and Wormit. Three or four men were required to feed each carpet into the beating machine, when a revolving drum with leather flails beat the carpet. One can only imagine the clouds of dust that would be produced by this treatment. When it was considered sufficiently beaten by the machine, the carpet was then removed and carried outside to be stretched out on the grass. The cleaning process was then completed by beating with brushes. After Harry Johnston retired in 1948 the business was taken over by his nephew William Willocks who kept it going for another twenty years.

Chemists

For over one hundred years four chemists served the pharmaceutical needs of the village, one of them, David Doig, operating for some 60 years. The chemist shop fronts

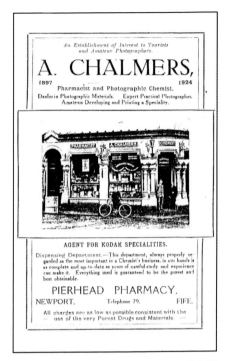

drum with leather flails beat the

Advert and view of Chalmers' shop at the pier.

144

Doig's first location at the top of the High Street.

In this advert Doig has moved to Robertson Place.

appeared on many old photographs. David Doig came from Dundee in 1876 and opened his chemist shop at No 1 High Street. By 1890 his two sons had joined him in the business. In the early 1900s they moved over the road to their Robertson Place (Cupar Road) shop (now in 2015 the optician) and David Doig and Sons operated there until the 1950s. At the turn of the century they also had a shop in Dundee. Meanwhile, down at the pier, Andrew Chalmers opened a chemist shop in the pier buildings and was in business there from 1897 until the 1940s. In the 1924 Newport guide, this shop was described as "an Establishment of Interest to Tourists and Amateur Photographers". In their pharmacy work everything used was guaranteed to be the purest and best available. This shop was then taken over by David Kerr. After the Doig family business ended, David Kerr took over the Robertson Place shop and for some time into the 1960s supervised both the shop there as well as the one at the pier. By the mid 1960s, perhaps seeing the writing on the wall for the pierhead shops resulting from the building of the road bridge, he vacated the pier shop to concentrate solely on the one in Robertson Place. When David Kerr retired in 1983 Ian Waugh then occupied the Robertson Place shop until 2004. When the chemist eventually in 2006 moved up to its new location beside the surgery, over one hundred years of a chemist presence in Robertson Place had come to an end.

Garages
John T Young was one of Newport's best-known business-men. He was the son of William Young who for many years at the turn of the twentieth century was the tenant of the Seamills smiddy at the pier-head. By 1896 John had established a successful cycle repair business on

This picture shows the extent of the J T Young garage by the 1950s.

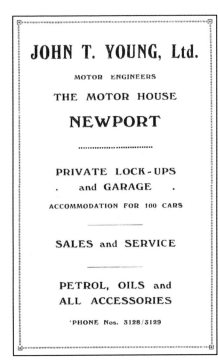

JOHN T. YOUNG, Ltd.

MOTOR ENGINEERS

THE MOTOR HOUSE

NEWPORT

....

PRIVATE LOCK - UPS
.   and GARAGE   .

ACCOMMODATION FOR 100 CARS

———

SALES and SERVICE

———

PETROL, OILS and
ALL ACCESSORIES

'PHONE Nos. 3128/3129

Services offered by J T Young.

the High Road. The new century however brought huge expansion as he embraced the new motor industry, and in the early 1900s he expanded down to Boat Road with the building of his garage there. Soon he was acknowledged as the local motoring expert, and after further rapid expansion on Boat Road the whole area below his cycle shed on the High Road would be occupied by his garage, workshop and showroom.

Motoring provided not only business but pleasure too. He was an honorary member of the Royal Scottish Automobile Club and his driving licence was one of the earliest issued by Fife County Council. In the 1920s his position in the motoring world was recognised by his peers when he was made

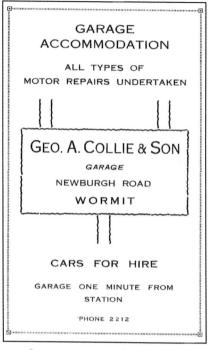

GARAGE
ACCOMMODATION

ALL TYPES OF
MOTOR REPAIRS UNDERTAKEN

GEO. A. COLLIE & SON
GARAGE
NEWBURGH ROAD
WORMIT

CARS FOR HIRE

GARAGE ONE MINUTE FROM
STATION

'PHONE 2212

Garage competition from Wormit.

president of the Scottish Motor Trades Association.

Throughout his life he played an active part in village affairs, being especially involved for many years in the cycling and curling clubs, for both of which he was secretary and treasurer. He was a member of Forgan Liberal Association, and he served on the Town Council almost continuously from 1919 until 1941. This included his service as Provost from 1931 until 1934. Interestingly, he was the first Provost to have been born and bred in Newport. He was also an Honorary Life Member of the Newport Club.

There was another very successful garage business in Wormit. Like J T Young, George Collie's motor and garage business developed from an earlier enterprise, but in his case it

The magnificent Collie's charabanc on an outing to Balmerino –
Balmerino Inn in the background.

147

James Johnstone's bus was the first to run between Newport and Tayport in the 1920s.

was from a stabling, horse-hiring and livery business. In the early 1900s he combined this with his first ventures into motor transport, but within a very few years he was concentrating on his motor business. From his premises on Naughton Road, now Don the blacksmith's workshop, he hired out cars, taxis and charabancs, and ran connecting bus services to the trains in Wormit and the ferries in Newport.

Gasworks
See Further Development of the Village P46.

Joiners
In the same way as the name Don in Newport means blacksmith, so the name Latto must mean joiner. Arthur Latto of Balmerino settled in Newport around 1840, and in the

late 1850s his son David became the first Latto joiner in the village. From the late 1860s David lived at Carseview (now 20 Tay Street) and in these early days had premises in the High Street. Among other work undertaken at this busy time in Newport's development, David assisted in the erection of Westwood, now St Serf's care home. By the 1880s his premises were in Union Street and he had extended his services to glazier and undertaker. David had two sons, James and John, who followed him into the business. James had no children, but John's son Herbert followed in his father's and grandfather's footsteps, and he in turn was followed by his son Michael. Although no longer occupying the Union Street premises, Michael continues to work part-time, and is proud to be the fourth generation of Latto joiners in the village.

Another long-established joinery business was Rankine's at Woodhaven. This firm was founded in 1875 by William Buist in the building above Woodhaven pier. Trade at the time was brisk in this area, and his men were fully employed both in the workshop and out on site benefiting from the boom in house building in the area in the last years of the nineteenth century. His grandson Willie Rankine joined the business in 1903 aged 13, eventually taking it over on his return from the Great War in 1919. His grandfather had given up two years earlier, aged 81! Like his grandfather, Willie worked on until well into his eighties, but passed the business on to his son Sandy in 1965. The sharp bend in the road at Woodhaven was always known as Rankine's corner. Sandy Rankine lived in the cottage there until the 1990s.

Laundry

Tayside Laundry.

Who can remember the Tayside Laundry? This was the red brick building situated on the Tayport Road, to the east of the present-day bridge road access, just beyond the road up to Northfeld farm. It operated from the early 1900s for some fifty years. No doubt this catchy slogan brought in lots of business!

On a green hill by the river
Where the gentle zephyrs blow
You should have your linen laundered
By the Tayside Laundry Co.

Technologically the Tayside Laundry was fairly advanced: from its opening in 1906 it was powered by electricity. The electricity was produced via the gas supply! A gas suction engine powered a dynamo, which in turn produced enough electricity to drive all the ironing machines and mangles, as well as supplying heating and lighting. After extensive research by the directors of the laundry it was discovered that this was by far the cheapest way of producing all the power required.

Plumbers

Betsworth and Barlow will be widely remembered as plumbers and gas fitters with premises on the north side of the High Street. The firm was started in 1894 by two local plumbers, John Barlow and Henry Betsworth, both aged 24. Interestingly both their fathers

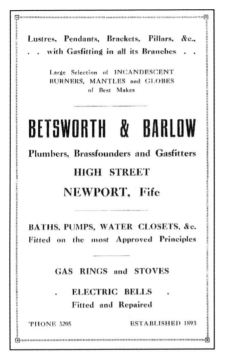

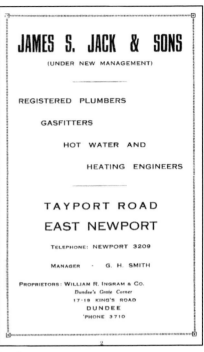

Adverts for plumbers.

worked on the Mars: Edward Betsworth was a naval instructor and John Barlow senior was a gymnastics instructor. Both families had moved here from England for the fathers to work on the ship. The 1891 census described John Barlow junior as a ship plumber so possibly he too had worked on the Mars. When the firm was started the two men decided whose surname would come first in the company name by the toss of a coin. Betsworth and Barlow started life in Gas Lane, but by 1905 had moved to the High Street. They soon became a household name in Newport.

Eventually John Barlow would buy out Mr Betsworth, and the business continued under three generations of John Barlow, father, son and grandson, until it closed in the late 1970s.

James Jack and Sons was another well known firm of plumbers and gasfitters in the village. James Jack had come to Newport from Brechin and started his business in 1880 on the High Street. By 1890 his workshop had moved to Union Street. In these early days as well as offering plumbing services, he was also described as a bellhanger. Two sons James and Robert followed him into the business. In the early 1900s he moved to Harp Cottage on Tay Street (now Little Beehive nursery) and operated a showroom in the premises attached while continuing with his Union Street workshop. In the 1930s and 1940s they also had premises in Bay Road, Wormit. From the 1950s until the 1980s James Jack and Sons continued in name only, still operating from the Union Street workshop but now run by George Smith. George Smith's sons and grandson still operate plumbing businesses in Newport today.

Post Office

The first Post Office in Newport was on the site where Trinity Church now stands. When this site was redeveloped around 1880 the Post Office moved down to the building opposite the pier where it would remain until after the ferry service ended in 1966. The building is easily recognised by the old stamp machines still in the wall. At the start of the twentieth century the post master was A M Anderson, better known as Postie Anderson. He was a man of many talents. As well as sorting the letters, he was a watchmaker, jeweller and optician, as advertised on the notices outside his shop and seen in old photographs. He was also a photographer of some repute, having taken many of the views of the village on the hundreds

Other services offered by postie Anderson, advertised above the Post Office doorway.

Rusting stamp machines, still on the old Post Office wall, have seen better days.

of different postcards which were produced before the First World War. These old postcards are an enormously valuable resource to us today, giving a wonderful view of the village at that time. Thank you Postie Anderson!

After the closure of the ferry service in 1966, the Post Office moved to the High Street, and after that to Cupar Road. Since 2014 it has been housed within the Spar shop on the High Street.

Wormit's Post Office opened in 1895 in what was the new building at the junction of Mount Stewart Road and Naughton Road, now the location of the Spar shop. After World War II it would move to its site on Naughton Road, west of The View restaurant.

The Post Office's recent relocation to within the Spar shop has taken the Post Office back to its original premises.

Salmon Fishing
See Early Development of the Village on page 21.

Ship-building at Woodhaven
Not many people are aware of the ship-building business at Woodhaven and I must thank William Owen for researching this subject. For six years between 1847 and 1853 Joseph Garland had a ship-building yard down beside the old pier. Garland had extensive ship-building experience behind him. He had served an apprenticeship before becoming a partner in a Dundee ship-building business in the 1830s. He followed this by operating his own yard at Newburgh from 1837 until 1846. His method of construction was simple: his timber ships were built in a depression in the ground, and when ready for launching, the depression was flooded and the ship floated out. Seven ships were built at Woodhaven, ranging in size from the 18 ton sloop Seagull to the 212 ton brig Remark. This was not ship-building on a large scale. In 1851 Joseph Garland employed only two other men and a few years later the business was no more. Joseph Garland continued to live in Newport after his business folded and maintained ownership of some of his ships.

Slaters and Roofers

John Storrier and Son. There can be few roofs in Newport and Wormit not closely examined by the Storrier family at one time or another! The first mention of Storriers as slaters dates to 1882 when Allan Storrier and John Storrier were described as slaters at the Pierhead. I can find no further mention of Allan, but John continued as a slater, moving his business in the 1890s to Union Street and living with his large family at Fountainbrae, Tay Street. We were fortunate at the last Old Newport exhibition in 2005 to have a photograph of this Storrier family. Three of his four sons (John, William and Herbert) became slaters. Sadly son Herbert would die in World War I. In 1910, the present business was established by John Storrier (son). Further generations followed. His son John Storrier jnr (actually the third John Storrier – slater) joined the business in the early 1920s. He was later joined by his eldest son, (John) Rankin Storrier, and in the 1940s the firm became John Storrier and Son. Following this, Rankin's brothers Alistair and later Douglas, joined them. From the late 1920s until around 1960 the business had bases in Wormit and Tayport as well as Newport. The business is now in the capable hands of Douglas and he is joined by Alistair's son Cammy and grandson Craig. This means that six generations of the family have been looking after the Newport roofs.

NEWPORT AT LEISURE

Over the years the people of Newport have developed a wide range of leisure activities. Some activities which started in the nineteenth century have continued through to the present day; others have faded in popularity and are almost forgotten.

Curling

The curling club was one of the earliest organised activities in the village. There had been an earlier club known as the Forgan Curling Club, but the Newport Curling Club was formed in 1858. They were fortunate to have two specially built curling ponds in the Tayfield grounds, and they soon had 80-90 members. The low pond was filled with water and therefore needed hard frost before it could be used. The upper pond was a concrete base which when covered with water could be used after quite a moderate frost. Invariably this rink had to be swept free of leaves before it could be flooded. In order to inform the members when the ice on the ponds was playable, the club was given permission in 1929 to hoist a flag on the Blyth Hall pole as a signal. In

Curling on the top pond in Tayfield. Curling house in the background.

NEWPORT CURLING CLUB
Instituted 30th January, 1858

CENTENARY YEAR

DINNER

Blyth Hall, Newport-on-Tay
Thursday, 30th January, 1958

CHAIRMAN · JOHN T. YOUNG

*This curling club dinner menu cover
gives a lovely picture of how the
curling ponds looked.*

of the lower pond until fairly recently. The curling club, although still in existence, ended their leasing of the Tayfield ponds in 1977, and they now have to go further afield to enjoy the Roaring Game. January 1985 saw the last curling by club members on the Tayfield ponds. In the 1970s the top curling pond was put to another use when cycling proficiency tests were held there. This was organised by Jim Smith, estate factor and also a special constable.

Bowling

In 1869 the Newport Bowling Club was founded and the Bowling Green was opened in 1877, money being raised for the new green by the sale of £1 shares. By 1890 the club had 100 members. Before the opening of the new bowling green in Scott Street, land in East Newport had been used. A bowling green was laid out on land feued from Seacraig House, which stood between King Street and Union Street where Seacraig Court houses now stand. After the new club and green had been set up, the old one continued to be used by the Maryton Bowling Club. The Newport Bowling Club continues to be one of the most popular and well-supported clubs in the village. Mr. Brown of the Newport Inn also had a bowling green in operation in the 1850's and 1860's. This green was laid out on the ground immediately opposite the

addition there were small notice boards in various parts of Newport saying 'Ice at Tayfield'. Access to the ponds for the curlers was by a little back gate, slightly to the west of the north lodge gate. The path up to the ponds was lit by two large gas lamps. At first the ponds were lit by oil and sometimes by flaming torchlight, but later by electricity from a World War I U-boat generator. This had been purchased and gifted to the club by J T Young, a keen curler and owner of the garage on Boat Brae. The brick-built club-house where members kept their stones was still there at the side

An early view of Newport Bowling Club from the 1880s.

Wormit Bowling Green with the original pavilion.

inn which later became the site for St. Mary's Church. Although it is now difficult to imagine how a flat bowling green could be fitted on this piece of ground, it is clearly described in an 1859 newspaper article. Wormit Bowling Club was established in 1901, with funds loaned by the members.

Tennis

The tennis club in Newport was established in 1884 and is in fact one of the oldest tennis clubs in Scotland. Their wooden pavilion was erected in 1903. The tennis club hosted frequent social events throughout the last century, with well attended dances and fancy dress balls in the Blyth Hall, and judging by the frequency of these occasions, members must have been as proficient at dancing as at tennis! There was also another tennis club in the village, the Seacraig Tennis Club. Early in the twentieth century they had a court laid out on the land which the Maryton Bowling Club had used. The Newport tennis courts now have an all weather surface and can be used all year round. In 1898 however the Dundee Courier reported a rather original suggestion that winter use might be

Dressed up to the nines at Newport tennis club in early 1900s.

Tennis tea at Newport in the 1950s.

The re-opening of Wormit Tennis Club in 1953.

made of the courts by flooding to allow ice skating. It is not known whether this idea was ever carried out.

In 1912 land at Bay Road was leased by the new Wormit Tennis Club to lay out their tennis courts. Although the club operated from that early date it went through a very weak period during and after World War II, with the town council planning to purchase the fairly derelict courts and club-house. In 1953 however the club was re-formed and they took over the existing courts. A new club-house was built in1961. In the late 1960s the courts were re-surfaced and

John and David Lloyd, eventually Britain's top male players, came along to play the opening match on the new surface. John would later become Wimbledon mixed doubles champion in 1983 and 1984. For some time in the 1970s popular Saturday night discos were held in the clubhouse.

Quoiting

Less well-known, in the top corner of Victoria Park, was the quoiting ground, home of the quoiting club. Set up in 1896, this club was very active until it finally expired in the 1930s. The triangular area used by the club is still fenced off, and can be

A quoiting match from 1913.

clearly seen. A substantial wooden club-house stood there. Quoiting required a great deal of skill and strength as it involved throwing heavy iron or steel rings (weighing between 2.7 and 5.5 kg) at a pin in the ground. The distance thrown was usually 20 metres. In the 1920s the quoiting club was holding well attended weekly dances in the small Blyth Hall.

Golf and Putting

Gone too is the putting green which between the two world wars occupied the ground beside Station Road and below Albert Crescent. Sadly the putting green became a casualty to the government's Dig for Victory campaign during World War Two, when all available land was taken over for food production. The village has not had a green since then.

Much to most people's surprise, Newport did at one time have a golf course. In the 1870s and 1880s there had been a course laid out on land near Inverdovat farm, but from the 1890s onwards members no longer had the use of the land, and so in 1891 the Newport Club joined with Scotscraig Golf Club at Tayport. The Newport course certainly had its limitations, consisting as it did of only six holes. For the annual competitions, three rounds had to be played. The club played for two medals: the Newport medal; and the Walker medal, presented by honorary captain Harry Walker (of Westwood, now St Serf's home) in

Wormit Bay Golf course.

1888. These two medals are still contested by Scotscraig Golf Club members. An 1890 issue of the Golfers' Annual magazine included a feature on the Newport Golf Club, and was less than complimentary about the quality of the course and the players. According to the article "the course is more famous for its magnificent view of mountain, sea and meadow than for the fine quality of its putting greens. The grass is long, the holes few in number and many are the strokes required to find them." It also suggested that if the view was not quite so beautiful the standard of play might improve. To improve the course the magazine suggested "the transportation of a few sand hillocks from Tentsmuir, and a bunker or two from St Andrews". After closure of the Inverdovat course hopes of a Newport Golf Club were not quite extinguished: in the Newport guide of 1924, strong suggestion was made of a course to be laid out on St Fort Estate. This plan surfaced again in 1938 when there is a reference in the burgh minutes to a possible course to the south of West Newport station. The approach of war no doubt gave the council more serious matters to address and the golf course plans came to nothing.

Wormit Bay Golf Club however was in existence from 1912 until 1940, when, like many others in the country, it was ploughed up to help with war-time food production. Part of the golf course land had originally been earmarked by the town council for football, but influential supporters of the golf course scheme argued strongly that a golf course would appeal to a wider age range, and they won the day. Much work was required on the land, and boys from the Mars training ship were asked to help clear the long weeds and stones. Although the Mars boys no doubt enjoyed this change of routine, and of course worked for no payment, as a thank-you gesture the golf club made a donation of five pounds to the Mars Boys Amusement Fund. The course had a lovely shore-side position down at Wormit Bay. In its 'Information for Members' booklet, it claimed to be the nearest golf course to Dundee city centre. From there, via the train, one could be on the first tee within fifteen minutes. By the mid-1920s membership had reached 200. During World War II when food supply lines from abroad were coming under daily attack the Government launched their Dig for Victory campaign which encouraged more home food production. As part of this campaign, many areas of land such as putting greens, bowling greens and golf courses were ploughed up, and Wormit Golf Course was one of the casualties. Sadly after the war the golf course was never reinstated.

Newport Braes

The Braes, which belonged originally to Tayfield estate, have been used for well over a hundred years as a public recreation ground. According to the burgh minutes of 1897, the burgh accepted management and control of the Braes for a rent of one pound per annum. They were officially gifted to the village in 1946 after which various amenities were added by the town council: paths, steps and seats. They were much enjoyed by both villagers and visitors. Indeed, for generations of Dundonians trying to escape the smoke and grime of the city, the Braes provided the perfect day trip destination, easily accessed by the Fifie. Local children were quick to seize the chance to make a penny or two on these occasions, as carelessly abandoned lemonade bottles were carefully collected and exchanged at the nearby shops in Royal Buildings for a few pence.

The Braes also provided a base for various water sports – see Swimming and Rowing below. In addition various other activities took place there, with newspapers describing open air church services in 1890, and musical promenades being held on summer evenings in 1875. In 1905 the splendidly named showman from Dundee Henry Marvello applied for permission to erect a stage and dressing room on

A busy day at the boat shed and slipway. Old Royal Buildings above.

the Braes so that he might provide evening entertainments during the summer months. In the past local children were always drawn to the beach: it was the ideal spot for sailing toy or home-made boats, paddling and just generally messing about in the water. They always knew when to head home for tea, as they could tell the time from the arrival and departure of the Fifies.

On special occasions, bonfires were lit at night on the large rock east of Big Rock, very often on regatta nights, but also on other important occasions such as coronations and other royal celebrations. This bonfire tradition had been started in the nineteenth century when fires were lit every year on 24 May to mark Queen Victoria's birthday. In these years before the First World War, British Summer Time had not been introduced, and so the summer evenings would be much darker than today, making the bonfire all the more impressive. Even more recently, in the 1950s and 1960s, it became a tradition to build a bonfire there for Guy Fawkes night, and indeed there was serious competition between the bonfire builders at the Braes and up at Craighead.

With steep slopes and swift currents, accidents inevitably happened, but sometimes with happy outcomes. On two separate occasions in 1891

The re-furbished Blyth fountain.

when children got into difficulties in the water, help arrived from a rather unexpected source. A black retriever dog called Bob, belonging to David McGregor who owned an eating establishment at Fountainbrae, now 24 Tay Street, immediately swam out into the water and pulled the child back to the shore. Bob was suitably rewarded by the Dundee Humane Society with a new collar. Later that same year, in two separate incidents at the same spot on the same day, two young men fell over the cliff to the rocky shore below. One man died instantly, while the other recovered from his injuries.

Also on the Braes is the drinking fountain, gifted to the village in 1882 by Mrs Blyth-Martin. Mrs Blyth-Martin lived at Blyth House, now 72 Tay Street, and she also gifted the Blyth Hall to the community in memory of her three brothers. The fountain is made of cast-iron and was produced by Walter Macfarlane and Co at the Saracen Foundry in Glasgow. It is fairly typical of fountains erected in the Victorian period, and closely resembles others still standing, some in far-flung corners of the world. At the time of its production, there was a widespread movement to provide clean drinking water whenever and wherever possible. It was also hoped that such provision would encourage habits of temperance. It is ironic that today such an open fountain is considered a health and

safety hazard and we are of course not now allowed to actually drink water from it! Since the fountain's extensive refurbishment in 2013 it is now well worth a close inspection. It is decorated with herons and stags, and inscribed with the reminder to "Keep the pavement dry". A further plaque states "The gift of Mrs Blyth-Martin 1882".

Today the Braes are a far cry from the busy, bustling area of the last century. On summer days they can be quite deserted, with only the occasional dog-walker enjoying the splendid views.

Swimming

For the people of Newport, the Braes provided an area to indulge in their favourite water sports, and they were home to both the bathing and boating clubs; both these clubs had premises there in the first half of the twentieth century. Strange as it may seem, one of Newport's attractions to its nineteenth century settlers was the fine sea bathing that it offered. The swimming club was in existence at least from the 1870s, possibly even earlier. The club had two changing sheds on the Braes, and a diving stage fifty yards west of the Big Rock. Swimming galas were held annually. The burgh council minutes of 1909 mention the possibility of a bathing pond being constructed at the Braes, but this was never achieved. The last club gala was held in 1928, and in 1930 the swimming

Everything necessary for a swim – two changing huts, an access ramp and a diving stand.

club itself folded. A few years later in 1934, the bathing huts, which were by then considered rather unsightly, and for which no further use had been found, were removed. The water however has always proved a great attraction, and even in the 1960s local youngsters could still be found regularly swimming down below the Braes. Margaret Wright remembers learning to swim there, with her mother watching from a nearby rock. Later she regularly got into trouble for swimming too far out. Her yellow bathing hat was easily spotted by her father who worked on the Fifie! How things have changed in the space of just one lifetime! Wormit Bay was also popular with swimmers, and in 1912 the town

council proposed positioning a line of floats along the bay there for swimmers' safety.

Rowing

In existence from 1866, Newport's rowing club was, in terms of membership, very quickly one of the biggest and most active in the village. When the Blyth Hall opened in 1877, John Leng remarked that "the curling club and bowling club could be accommodated in the small hall, but the rowing club, I expect, will need the larger one". The club continued as the Newport Boating Club until the 1920s. Membership of the club was badly affected during World War I with the loss of several members. The boat club had a boat shed and slipway on the east side of

Plenty water activity here with spectators enjoying every precarious vantage point.

Big Rock, and James Scrymgeour remembered that on summer evenings "there were always young fellows down there messing about with their boats". Like the swimming club galas, boat club regattas were held annually, although in the early years there had been two regattas, one held in the autumn. In the 1870s the regatta had been contested by a crew of young engineers employed in the building of the first Tay railway bridge. Races in the regattas were from Big Rock to half-way to Woodhaven Pier. Crews came from Broughty Ferry, Dundee and Arbroath. The Mars training ship sent a crew and the local Boys' Brigade entered their boat. On these special days, local confectioners took advantage of the crowds and set up their ice cream barrows and stalls with brightly coloured awnings, which often stretched from the High Street to Robert Street. The Mars boys' band would play throughout the afternoon, grouped around the fountain. The boating club also organised annual outings, very often a cruise up-river on a chartered steamboat. In 1896 they cruised to Bridge of Earn. Tea was served on deck, and some time was spent ashore when a group photograph was taken. On the return sail of three hours, an impromptu concert was enjoyed. Another highlight of the club year was the annual procession, when as many boats as possible gathered to parade across the river and along the Dundee shore.

Other Sports

The more traditional ball games of football, cricket, rugby and even hockey have also been well supported. Newport has always fielded a football team and indeed

Local football team from the 1970s.

Newport 3rd cricket team from 1910.

Hockey team from 1912.

the Newport Amateurs Football Club can trace its origins back to 1922. They now play and train at Waterstone Crook, but previously their home ground was Windmill Park. In the 1960s/1970s Newport also fielded a successful ladies' football team, still fondly remembered by the players. According to the 1924 guide to Newport, both ladies' and gentlemen's hockey teams played at Windmill Park. When Waterstone Crook was first offered as a recreation area by William Berry in 1900, both cricket and rugby pitches were laid out there. Later, in 1925, the burgh minutes mention the cricket pitch in Windmill Park. With the exception of football of course, it appears that these games are no longer participant sports in Newport.

Temperance Association

The Temperance Movement had a strong following in the first half of the 20th century in Scotland. Like many towns, both Newport and Wormit had their local temperance groups and a Band of Hope for the children. Perhaps the temperance support in this area was strengthened in 1922, when Dundee elected the first, and last, temperance MP, Edwin "Neddy" Scrymgeour, who fought the election on a prohibition standpoint, incidentally ousting no less a personality than Winston Churchill.

Churchill had been MP for Dundee since 1908. He left, vowing never to return to the city. He never did return, even after the end of World War Two when as a national hero he was offered the freedom of the city. At the Newport Temperance Society meetings, magic lanterns and glass slides would be used so that everyone could sing along to the hymns. The members of the Temperance Association and the children of the Band of Hope took a life-long pledge to shun the evils of alcohol. How many kept their promise?

Recreation Park

At the start of the twentieth century the village recreation ground was at Waterstone Crook. This ground had been offered by William Berry in 1900 for use by the football, rugby and cricket clubs. In 1906 a refreshment room and a dressing room were provided there, and a local baker was also given permission to set up a refreshment stall at busy times. In 1907 however the burgh minutes reported 'rowdyism' at Waterston Park, and by 1908 a policeman was needed to maintain order on Saturday afternoons. It was decided therefore that no more permission would be given for picnic parties or sports teams from outwith the village to play there.

From 1910 onwards a lease was negotiated with Tayfield for the new Windmill Park. Situated beyond where the dual carriageway now runs, the park was reached by a path at the top of Victoria Street, and was named for the windmill which stood at the south end of the park. Windmill Park was officially opened on Coronation Day in June, 1911, when a ceremonial gold key was presented to Provost William Robertson: the key would later be returned by the Robertson family to the town council. The new park was at first very stony but local boys cleared the stones for a penny a bag! It was further improved by the generosity of William Leng of Highfield, who donated £500 for the laying out and fencing of the new ground; his generosity was perhaps to some extent a reflection of his relief at the recreation park no longer being next to his home at Waterstone Crook! Subscriptions were collected locally and a pavilion was erected at the new park: this provided changing rooms for the sports participants. The park would be used for football, hockey (men and women), rugby and cricket. Windmill Park would prove enormously popular for the next half century, not only with local people, but also with visitors from Dundee over on the Fifie or the train for a day out. It was especially popular as a Sunday-school picnic venue, and when local children were not collecting discarded lemonade bottles on the Braes, they scoured Windmill Park for money dropped by careless picnickers. Its popularity also proved a disadvantage on occasions, especially in the early days. Like Waterstone Park, it sometimes proved just too popular, and there were frequent complaints about the drunkenness and rowdiness of some of the visitors...... although presumably not the Sunday-school picnickers! In an attempt to calm the situation, in 1914 local pubs were encouraged to close early on Dundee holidays to discourage visitors: no doubt an unpopular move with locals as well as visitors, but something they would have to get used to anyway under wartime licensing restrictions.

With the building in the 1960s of the Tay Road Bridge and its connecting dual carriageway, the town council realised the impracticalities and dangers of Windmill Park's position. They therefore set about improving the play-park in Gowrie Woods by installing new equipment there. At the same time they developed a completely new park in the field behind Kinbrae. But even after the construction of the new road, Windmill Park continued to be used. Margaret Wright remembers escorting classes of primary school classes up to the park for sports/PE, with the traffic on the dual carriageway being halted to allow the children to cross!

In 1975 the village acquired another recreation area when the lease for Victoria Park was offered by Dr John Berry.

Winter Sports

Being built on a hill, Newport and Wormit have always provided splendid opportunities for fast downhill sledging, and local youngsters have enthusiastically taken full advantage of annual snowfall. Inevitably in the past when there was little motor traffic, much of this activity took place in the streets. Certain streets were favourites: Kilnburn was always most popular, with James Street, Gowrie Street, Castle Brae and Shepherd's Brae running close seconds. Even in the traffic-free streets of 1908 this was considered dangerous and in that year six 'respectable lads' were up before the Burgh Police Court for sledging in Kilnburn. Because street-sledging was widespread in the burgh handbills were issued to the residents reminding everyone that 'sledging, tobogganing, skating and sliding on the streets are contraventions of the Burgh Police (Scotland) Act 1892'. Despite the council's resolve in 1908 that there should be no more sledging in the streets, they fought a losing battle as this activity continued. Some of our older residents have happy memories of sledging down Kilnburn, down the steps and on down Boat Brae. An alternative and equally exciting route was from Norwood down Craighead Crescent and on down James Street to Tay Street.

Before the modern 1980s and 1990s houses were built on the south side of the main road at Woodhaven, the sloping field there was popular for sledging. The intrepid sledger, if going fast enough, could speed out the gate, across the main road, and down the track to Woodhaven pier. Nowadays sledging is mainly confined to Victoria and Kinbrae parks. In Wormit a favourite spot is the school field but in the past the steep curves of Flass Road provided an irresistible attraction.

Although recent milder winters seem to have ended the tradition of outdoor skating, in the past this was much enjoyed. As soon as word spread that the ice was 'bearing', local youngsters headed up to the Causewayhead Farm pond to skate. They also skated in Tayfield, both on the top duckpond and on the curling ponds when no curling was planned.

Music and Drama

The less energetic of a musical disposition could at one time spend their leisure moments with the Newport Operatic Society, which in the 1920s and 1930s enjoyed a great rivalry with other local operatic societies, and Ron Caird remembers Operatic Society shows in the Blyth Hall. For one show it was decided that the gas lights in the hall were not sufficient and so a threshing machine was borrowed from a local farm, and was set up outside the hall

where it generated electricity. At the parts of the show where more lighting was required the thresher had to work so hard it was quite impossible for anyone to hear the show. Even earlier a Musical Society had also met in the Blyth Hall in winter months. One could also join the Orchestral Society or sing with the Choral Society which, at the turn of the last century, held rather grand events in the Blyth Hall at which evening dress was encouraged! The Choral Society won much praise over a wide area, and their ambitious shows and concerts earned them glowing reports in the Dundee press. Sadly the departure of many of the male singers on the outbreak of World War I led to the Society's disbandment, and it was not re-formed afterwards. In the 1970s and 1980s the Townswomen's Guild also had a choir which won prizes in national competitions. The Guild also had a very enthusiastic drama group.

The Orchestral and Choral Societies may now just be distant memories but since World War II there have been several musical and dramatic groups to join. In the 1960s there were two drama groups in the village, the Blythe Players and the Green Room Club. The Blythe Players as their name suggests put on their shows in the Blyth Hall (with that surprising 'e' in their name), performing such favourites as Agatha Christie's The Hollow

The operatic society posing outside the Blyth Hall in 1930s.

(1959) and Charley's Aunt (1964). The Green Room Club met and practised in their premises in Royal Buildings before performing in the Rio. These two groups eventually combined to become the Phoenix Drama Club. Since the 1950s TAMS (Tayport Amateur Musical Society) has had a strong association with Newport, practising and performing in the Blyth Hall as well as in Dundee and Tayport. Now re-named TADAMS (Tayport Amateur Dramatic and Musical Society) they continue to entertain.

Budding juvenile thespians weren't forgotten, as TNT (The Newport Theatre) catered for them. For more than twenty-five years from the early 1980s until 2007 hundreds of local youngsters were able to show off their talents in shows such as the Dracula Spectacular, Tin Pan Alley and The Lion, the Witch and the Wardrobe. TNT was one of the earliest youth theatre groups, and certainly the first in this area. Always ambitious, they very often put on shows which other groups might not attempt. Their first show was Rock, and their final one Bugsy Malone. Money raised was donated to local and children's charities.

Men's Clubs (and Women's!)
The Newport Club, popular meeting

place of the men of the village, and based in their club-rooms above the High Street shops, has a long history. The club was founded as the West Newport Club in 1871 by some of the engineers and men working on the first railway bridge, as a place to pass their leisure hours. The club first met in the upper floor premises of the building at 35/37 West Road, the building which had earlier been used as the Congregational Chapel. In 1894 they moved to their new premises at 1 St Phillan's Place above the High Street, and at that time took the new name the Newport Club. In 1949 the Club purchased the premises. From the start the club provided their members with a place to relax. Many came for a quiet drink and for fellowship with other members, or to play billiards or cards. In the earlier years the reading room was always popular, with an astonishing selection of magazines being provided, in addition to morning and evening newspapers. Nowadays the Club still boasts around 40 members, and, as well as continuing to enjoy the club facilities, members appreciate the excellent company and the relaxed atmosphere. New members are always welcome!

There was also for many years at the start of the twentieth century a working men's club which met in St Mary's Church hall. Highly popular penny concerts were held there on Saturday evenings. Sometimes the Mars boys provided the entertainment, and James Scrymgeour also remembered a highly talented ventriloquist.

More recently, since World War II, the men of the village have been attracted to Rotary, to Round Table and to Probus.

Rotary is of course well known for its community work, charitable events, and other fundraising activities. The Rotary Club of North Fife was formed in 1969, initially as an extension of Dundee Rotary. The club's 29 founder members came from the villages of Tayport, Newport, Wormit, Gauldry and Balmerino. In these early days meetings were in the Sandford Hotel, and from the outset North Fife Rotary was unusual in holding evening meetings, as most other Rotary Clubs met at lunch-time. Indeed the club was one of the first to be based on the place of residence rather than the place of work. Meetings have always followed the same format with a meal, a talk by a speaker, and business discussed. A huge milestone in Rotary history came in 1989 when it was agreed to admit women to this traditionally male organisation. North Fife Rotary's first lady members joined in 2002, and although now in 2016 the club has its first lady President, female membership has never been high. Meetings are now held in Scotscraig Golf Club. The North Fife club has participated in and contributed to all the major Rotary International initiatives and campaigns. These include helping towards the eradication of polio in most of the world today, and supporting the Shelterbox project which aims to deliver substantial shelters, housing 10 persons each, to the scene of any disaster within days. In addition they have supported a host of local and international charities, and do their utmost to promote community spirit by becoming involved in all sorts of community events. In 1981 a local branch of Inner Wheel was formed, with membership open to wives of Rotarians. Inner Wheel continues to support Rotary in their charitable and community work, while also supporting its own charities. There has been a wide range of fund-raising activities including fashion shows, a charity shop, and an open gardens scheme. Inner Wheel currently meets monthly in St Michael's Inn, and members no longer require the Rotary connection.

Newport-on-Tay (Scotscraig) Round Table was inaugurated in 1967. Membership was open to men aged 16 to 40, later extended to 45. Round Table was hugely popular in this area, with its highest membership in the 1970s and 1980s. The group met at various times in the Seymour Hotel, the Newport Hotel, the Brig o' Tay and the Sandford Hotel. They held regular social events for members, including dances, Burns Suppers, and even family weekends away. The annual bonfire and firework display organised for the village was greatly anticipated every year, and always much enjoyed. For some years there was an active Ladies Circle group, the associated organisation for members' wives. Round Table also raised large sums of money for various charities. One of their earliest fund-raising efforts was the setting up of an Antiques Shop on three Saturdays in a vacant shop on Cupar Road. Good quality jumble and other suitable items for sale were collected around the village in the days prior to the sale. This must surely be Newport's first pop-up shop! Fund-raising Summer Fairs were also held in the grounds of Tayfield. A tree was presented and planted there in 1971 as a thank-you to Dr and Mrs Berry for allowing the use of the grounds. The tree can still be seen near the old bee house, although the presentation plaque has now been removed for safe-keeping. In 1969 the end of the rail service between Newport and Dundee was suitably recognised. Table members dressed in mourning clothes and carried a coffin on the last train to leave Newport. Sadly falling membership numbers led to Round Table's inevitable closure in 2001.

In the 1970s an XT club was formed by ex-Round Table members who had exceeded the age limit. This group still meets monthly in St Michaels Inn.

Until recently there were two Men's Probus groups meeting in Newport. The aims and concept of Probus was to make provision for "the regular meeting of retired PROfessional and BUSiness men for friendly social intercourse and to relieve the isolation of retirement". The first group, the Probus Club of North Fife, was established in 1972. Meetings were initially held in Sandford Hill Hotel, and then moved to the Servite lounge at Kinbrae in 1985. This group proved very popular and grew rapidly. Membership reached 40, and a waiting list was formed.

Because of Probus' popularity, the Probus Club of Newport-on-Tay was formed in 1992 and still meets fortnightly in Newport Church Hall. This new club very quickly also had 40 members. In the early years some of their meetings hosted guest speakers, while some were "devoted to the strengthening of friendship through conversation and circulation". Members desired outings, golf and bowling matches. Visits were therefore made to Glenturret Distillery, Torness Nuclear Power Station, Verdant Works, Fife Police HQ and RAF Leuchars. They also visited Scotscraig Golf Club annually for golf and high tea.

In 1998 North East Fife Ladies' Probus Club was started. This still meets monthly in the church hall.

In 2000 the millennium was celebrated with a dinner/entertainment in the Blyth Hall, attended by members of all three Probus groups. In recent years joint meetings of all the local Probus groups have been held annually in December.

Blyth Hall

The Blyth Hall is a venue for various concerts and shows, and over the years has been home to many clubs and societies. Badminton has been played there fairly regularly since 1927, with the beautifully sprung floor providing a superb base for this sport. Upstairs in the small Blyth Hall the Annandale Bridge Club has met weekly since 1949, and is still going strong in 2016. The club is named after the house at Woodhaven where it was formed. With over 40 members at present, the bridge club is in a healthy position, and must surely be one of the longest running users of the hall. A Chess Club and a Literary and Debating Society have also met in the small hall. Country dancing classes, the old people's club, keep fit classes and playgroup have all been based here. In the 1930s a Horticultural Society was organised, and they held an annual show in the hall.

The local library is also based in the hall. Newport's first library was organised by the Free Church in their hall in William Street in the middle of the nineteenth century. In 1869 Newport Public Library was

A well-attended dance in the Blyth Hall late 1940s. Photograph taken from the gallery.

started by several Newport gentlemen. First located in the Congregational Church hall it then transferred to the Blyth Hall when the offices were built at the rear in 1890. The library later moved into the school next door, and finally back to its present location in the Blyth Hall. Since 2009 the Heritage Centre has been part of the library and is well worth a visit for anyone interested in Newport's past.

In addition to the above clubs and societies, the hall has been used for weddings and family celebrations, ceilidhs and dances, coffee mornings and sales, displays and exhibitions, and of course.....Old Newport Exhibitions!

The Rio Cinema

Now the community centre in St Mary's Lane, the Rio Cinema opened in 1939. At the height of its popularity the cinema programme changed three times weekly. Monthly programmes were produced, and posted out to regular attenders. Season tickets were also offered. In October 1955 prices ranged from 6d (2½p) up to 2/6 (12½p), and 25 films were shown including The Colditz Story and Above Us the Waves. By July 1963, prices had risen to 9d (4p) up to 3/6 (17½p), but even big hits like South Pacific and Elvis Presley's Girls Girls Girls couldn't save the Rio. Lack of patronage meant it followed the general trend of cinema closures, and it closed in 1963, the final film

*Cover page of the monthly
Rio programme leaflet.*

shown being Hatari, a John Wayne movie about African wildlife. After closure the Rio was used briefly as a furniture repository before becoming a youth club in 1969. In 1975 it became a community centre. The centre has a large hall plus other meeting rooms which can be hired. The computer room has computers available for community use, and classes in computing are also offered. Over the last forty years the Rio has hosted coffee mornings, dances, jumble and other sales, and has offered a wide range of classes from languages to creative writing to researching family history. Activity clubs and meeting groups have been held for all ages from pre-school through to the over-60s. Recently a touch of nostalgia has been introduced with the occasional showing of vintage films: this takes the Rio right back to its roots!

Waterston Crook

Waterston Crook sports centre opened in 1975 and provides fine facilities for a number of sports. Construction of the centre however was beset with problems: twice the squash court walls collapsed in high winds. At first the sports hall was housed within an air dome, and it was certainly not an unqualified success. During February 1980 it collapsed under the weight of snow on the roof, and in January 1984 it was again destroyed, this time by gales. After this second disaster, the air dome was replaced with a permanent structure.

Youth Groups

All the usual youth organisations have had branches in Newport and Wormit. In 1923 a Girl Guide company was started in Newport with the Brownies following soon after. Newport Guides were able to celebrate 60 years in 1983, and in 1985 celebrated the 75th anniversary of the Guiding movement. A Guide company and Brownie pack were soon established in Wormit too. In the 1960s a Ranger group met in Newport, catering for older girls. At the present time there is no Newport Guide company, but the Wormit

The Maharajah of Kallimpoor arrives at Wormit – see Youth Groups.

company meets in the Scout HQ at Waterstone Crook and welcomes members from both Newport and Wormit. A very active Brownie group meets in Newport, and another in Wormit. There is also a joint Newport/Wormit Rainbow group for younger girls.

Scout companies and Cub packs were formed here possibly as early as 1914. The Scouts were first registered as the 16th Dundee Scout Group, but in 1934 they were re-registered as 34th Fife. After the Mars training ship left in 1929, the Scouts took over part of the Mars sheds on Woodhaven Pier as their headquarters. In order to raise funds to purchase and repair their new HQ in 1933 the Scouts staged a major fund-raising exercise. They organised a fair where the guest of

honour was the Maharajah of Kallimpoor, who arrived at Wormit by train from Dundee with his four wives and other attendants. The Maharajah's name (Call Him Poor) was of course a play on words and the stunt did succeed in its fund-raising aims. The Scouts were based down at Woodhaven until after World War II, although during the war they had to vacate the premises to allow occupation by the Norwegian troops stationed there. During the war years the Scouts met in Newport School. They returned briefly to the Mars sheds but by 1948 had moved to new premises at the top of Kinbrae Park. The wooden hut there was ex-army, previously used to house prisoners-of-war near Ladybank, and purchased by the Scouts following a fund-raising drive. These premises served until the 1980s when a further fund-raising campaign led to the construction of the new Scout Hut next to Waterstone Crook sports centre. This new hut opened in 1987. There have also been very active Boys' Brigade companies in both Newport and Wormit. There is a very early photograph of the Newport company outside the Blyth Hall in 1901, but the company was officially registered in 1926, and has been in existence since then. A group for younger boys soon followed: these were the Lifeboys, later re-named the Junior Section.   In the early 1980s five-to-seven-year-olds were catered for with the formation of an Anchor Boys group.

A Wormit company was established in the post-war years, and for many years both companies attracted large numbers of boys at every level. Now the Newport and Wormit companies have combined.

Forgan Arts Centre

Since Forgan School closed in the early 1970s the building has been used as an Arts Centre. This has proved a wonderful amenity for Newport and has provided a great range of day and evening classes. These have included painting and drawing, pottery, upholstery, furniture restoration, stained glasswork, knitting, sewing and other needlework, bridge, photography and even cycle maintenance.

Newport Pipe Band in the 1930s.

179

Other Activities

A few other activities have been popular in the past. Early in the twentieth century pleasure steamers plied up and down the river, many of them stopping at Newport to land and take on passengers. From 1909 until 1923 the Miniature Rifle Club met at their rifle range down below the High Street. There was also at some time a Rifle Club in Wormit. Also before WWI an early Camera Club was formed in the village, with premises on the High Street. In the 1930s Newport had a very successful Pipe Band which was always in attendance at any public events. In old cine film of the 1937 Coronation celebrations, the Pipe Band can be seen leading the procession to the park. Disbanded during World War II it was never re-formed.

And Finally...
(Just not sure where in the book this should go – so here it is!)

Mercury and Maia

In October 1938 some unusual activity could be seen out on the river, and local children were allowed out of school to view the action from the Kilnburn steps. The Tay had been chosen as the starting point for a remarkable journey, and one that would go down in aeronautical history. This journey would involve two seaplanes, the Mercury and the Maia, and the flight destination was South Africa. A journey of that distance was considered in the 1930s too far for any seaplane: the vast amounts of fuel required for both take-off and for the long journey would be far too heavy for any seaplane at that time. The solution was simple. Two planes would be used and one would ride piggy-back for the take-off, thus conserving vital fuel supplies for the long flight ahead.

On 6th October the Maia flying boat took off from the River Tay with the Mercury seaplane on its back. The two planes separated a few miles beyond the city, and the Mercury headed off to Africa. Some forty-two hours later Mercury descended through a cloud of flamingos and touched down on the River Orange in Alexander Bay, South Africa. Captain Donald Bennett had set a world distance record of non-stop flight of 6,045 miles for a seaplane, a record that still stands today. Sadly Maia was destroyed by German bombers while moored in Poole Harbour, Dorset in 1941.

Mercury and Maia on the Tay before their record breaking flight.

SOME DATES OF INTEREST

1124	Founding of the old Kirk at Forgan
12th and 13th centuries	The earliest references to ferries over the Tay
14th century	Probable date of the old Forgan Kirk
16th century	the Seamills leased by Dundee magistrates
1713	Land around the Seamills bought by Dundee Guildry
1788	John Berry bought land and formed the Tayfield Estate
1790	Turnpike road built to Woodhaven
1808	Turnpike road built to Newport
1821	First steamship, The "Union", introduced on ferry crossing
1823	Construction of new pier for new steam ferries
1830	New road to east and west of Newport completed
1841	New Forgan Kirk opened
1848	Railway link from Leuchars to Tayport
1856	Gas company formed and first gasworks built below the High Street
1877	Blyth Hall opened
1878	First railway bridge opened
1879	Newport school opened
1879	Tay Bridge disaster
1887	Newport becomes a burgh
1887	Opening of second railway bridge
1896	Wormit School opened

SOME DATES OF INTEREST

1902	Burgh boundaries extended to include Woodhaven and Wormit
1903	New gasworks built on Tayport road
1911	Windmill Park opened
1937	Silver Jubilee of burgh
1939	Rio Cinema opened
1950 and 1958	Royal visits to Newport
1960	School becomes primary only
1966	Closure of railway line from Newport to Tayport
1966	Road bridge opened and ferry service ended
1969	Railway and stations closed
1975	Opening of Waterston Crook sports centre
1975	Local government reorganisation: end of town council
1977	New primary school built on outskirts of village
1978	New surgery built in Victoria Street
2006	Rebuilding of surgery/health centre
2013-2016	Refurbishment of Newport Hotel

POPULATION

	Parish of Forgan	Newport Village
1801	916	—
1811	898	—
1821	937	—
1831	1090	—
1841	1219	584
1851	1125	580
1861	1326	719
1871	2243	1507
1881	3308	2311
1891	3763	2545
1901	4720	2869
1911	4771	3643*
1921	3852	3320*
1931	3810	3275*
1951	3727	3274*
1961	3581	3324*
1971	3948	3719*
1981	3890	3652*
1991		4150*
2001		4304*
2011		4243*

figures include Wormit after 1902

SOURCES

History of Newport: J S Neish (published W and D C Thomson, 1890)

Old Statistical Account: 1793

New Statistical Account: 1838

3rd Statistical Account: 1952

Newport-on-Tay Burgh Minutes 1897-1975
(held in St Andrews University Library)

The Evolution of the Mars Ship: Captain A. L. Scott, 1917
(kindly lent by Mr. Jack Scott)

The High Girders: John Prebble

The Fall of the Tay Bridge: David Swinfen

The Mars Training Ship: Linda McGill

We'll Send Ye Tae the Mars: Gordon Douglas

Tales of Newport: James T Scrymgeour

The Buildings of Scotland – Fife: John Gifford

Newport Curling Club – year by year 1858-2010:
Researched by Jennifer Ferguson

Jim Smith's lifetime recollections, especially of Tayfield estate and also of life in the village, carefully noted by Gordon Small

Courier/Advertiser/People's Journal news articles

Forgansfields website: Nigel Clark

Newport Club website

Twentytwoflassroad website: William Owen